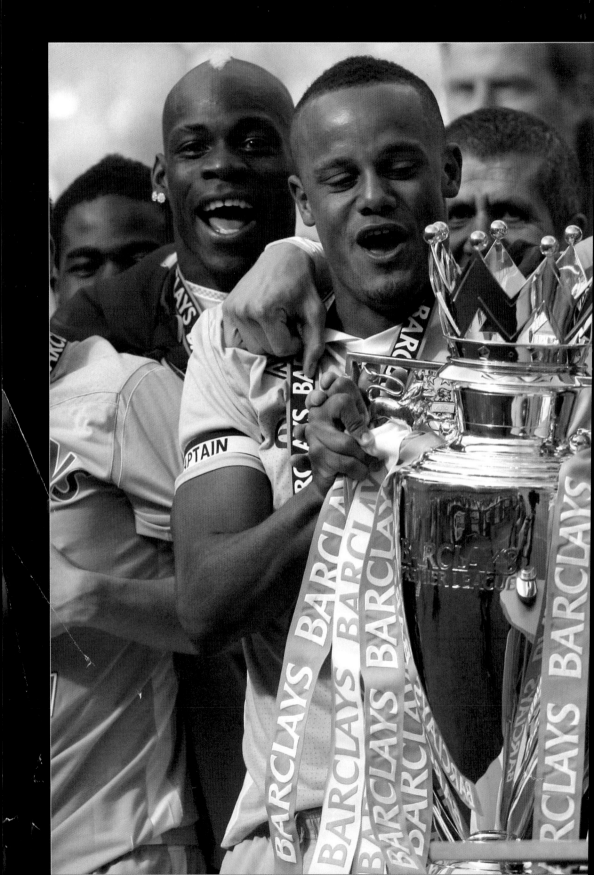

CONTENTS

Your guide to the best players, the biggest legends, top competitions and the winners of all the major football events on the planet. Statistics are correct until the end of season 2011-12. Where there are disputed figures we have relied on official records and club historians for help.

Published 2012.

Pedigree Books Limited, Beech Hill House, Walnut Gardens, Exeter, Devon EX4 4DH
www.pedigreebooks.com | shoot@pedigreegroup.co.uk

The Pedigree trademark, email and website addresses, are the sole and exclusive properties of Pedigree Group Limited, used under licence in this publication.

THE BEAUTIFUL GAME!

WE JUST LOVE IT!

IS THERE ANYTHING BETTER THAN FOOTBALL?

Around the planet fans can have their own opinions on how football should be played, their own views on every match they have watched.

We often disagree, even with our closest mates, about which player should be picked and who has played good or bad for our favourite side.

Heads might fall when our favourite side gets beaten. But it doesn't last long. Even the worse derby day defeat seems a long way off after a stunning victory in the next game.

So how did all of this start?

Where it all began...

Football is more than 2,000 years old!

It wasn't football as we know it, of course. There were probably very few rules, certainly no referees to criticise and no magnificent stadia.

But it was a game, with a round ball, played between teams. The players would probably have kicked and held the ball to run with it and their aim would be to score a goal.

Around 300 years BC there are records of ball games being played by Greeks and Romans and over the next centuries various forms of what we now know as football developed around the world.

Although England is widely acknowledged as the country that gave football its first set of proper rules, some of the earliest instances of the game can be traced back to Japan and Korea.

Progression

The word football is first recorded in the early 1400s by King Henry IV.

There are reports that King Henry VIII even ordered a pair of football boots in the 1500s – although they were most certainly not from one of today's manufacturers and didn't carry blades or studs!

Various games involving balls developed over the next two centuries but it wasn't until the late 1700s that real football started to take shape, although there were many different rules in different parts of the country and around the world.

Modern day

Although it was still a long, long way off what we now watch every week, football really began taking shape in England in 1863 when a number of school bodies got together to create the basic set of rules which we still use today.

The Football Association was formed at this time and handed the responsibility of looking after the game in England.

It was the first association of its kind and led to other bodies being formed around the world, notably the International Football Association Board in 1886, which would include the FAs of Scotland, Wales and Northern Ireland plus FIFA, the international governing body of the game.

FIFA itself wasn't formed until 1904 and brought together Belgium, Denmark, France, Holland, Portugal, Madrid FC, Sweden, Switzerland and Germany.

The first World Cup followed in 1930 and from then on the game developed into the global sport that is now played in virtually every corner of the planet.

and now...

You can check out the facts, figures and stats packed into the following pages of this yearbook. They are up to date as of the end of season 2011-12.

Some of the records will never be beaten. Some are there to be marvelled at forever.

Welcome again to the wonderful history of football...

THE
TEAMS
YOUR GUIDE TO THE SIDES

Grounds, star players, history, nicknames

Premier League // **Championship** // League One // **League Two**
Scottish Premier // **Conference** // Top world and European sides

Arsenal

Thierry Henry

Founded: 1886   **Ground:** Emirates Stadium
Capacity: 60,350   **Nickname:** Gunners

HONOURS

League Champions: 1931, 1933, 1934, 1935, 1938, 1948, 1953, 1971, 1989, 1991, 1998, 2002, 2004
FA Cup: 1930, 1936, 1950, 1971, 1979, 1993, 1998, 2002, 2003, 2005
League Cup: 1987, 1993
Inter Cities Fairs Cup: 1970
European Cup Winners' Cup: 1994

Arsenal moved from their famous Highbury ground to the impressive Emirates Stadium in summer 2006. Despite their ultra-modern ground they are still one of the most historic clubs in England.

They are noted for playing attractive football and their French boss Arsene Wenger has made them a joy to watch. Yet before he took over the Gunners in 1996, Arsenal were often dubbed boring as they often won games 1-0. Wenger is one of the most highly rated coaches in the game and is the Gunners longest-serving and most successful manager.

PLAYERS

Most appearances:
David O'Leary (1975-93) 722
Premier League:
Ray Parlour (1992-04) 333
Republic of Ireland defender O'Leary spent 20 years with Arsenal before moving to Leeds. He joined the club as a schoolboy and made his name as a cool, calm and skilled central defender for both club and country. Midfielder Parlour was an unsung hero for the Gunners, but was recognised by fans for his hard work.

Most goals:
Thierry Henry (1999-07, 2012) 228
The France striker was a winger when he arrived at Highbury for £10m from Juventus in 1999. But after being converted to a striker – who also operated out wide – he became a smash hit with supporters. Speed and incredible finishing made Henry a nightmare for defenders but a dream fro Arsenal fans. Henry was sold to Barcelona for £16m in 2007 before joining New York Red Bulls in summer of 2010, returned on loan in January 2012. The club's record goalscorer with 228 goals in 376 appearances.

Fan Favourite: Alex Oxlade-Chamberlain
The teenage winger joined Arsenal from Southampton for an initial fee of £12m in 2011 and is already a firm favourite with the fans. He's expected to blossom into an important winger or central midfielder over the next few years. He's broken through into the full England side from the Under-21s.

Alex Oxlade-Chamberlain

ARSENAL

AVFC
PREPARED

PLAYERS

Most appearances:
Charlie Aitken (1959-76) 657
Premier League:
Gareth Barry 385 (1997-09)
The England midfielder joined Villa from Brighton and became a firm fans favourite until his move to Man City in summer 2009. He was just 16 when he moved to the Midlands and played in central defence, left back and in midfield, eventually becoming the side's captain.

Most goals:
Billy Walker (1919-33) 244
Premier League:
Dwight Yorke 60 (1989-98)
Striker Yorke cost Villa nothing after they spotted him during a tour of the West Indies but earned them £12.6m when he was sold to Man United. The natural predator with a great finish was very popular at Villa Park but his stock fell when he joined United and later when he moved to arch-rivals Birmingham City.

Fan Favourite: Gabby Agbonlahor
The Birmingham-born striker-winger has speed and power and has now captained his local side. Had short spells on loan to Watford and Sheffield Wednesday early in his career but has now played more than 250 games for the Villans averaging almost a goal every four games.

Dwight Yorke

Villa were one of the founding members of both the Football League and the Premier League.

Although they have a fine haul of domestic trophies – one of the biggest in the land – their biggest moment was the European Cup victory over Bayern Munich in 1982.

Burly striker Peter Withe scored the only goal of that game to make Villa one of only four English sides to win Europe's biggest domestic competition. They beat Barcelona the following year to earn the European Super Cup.

Premier League runners-up at the end of the competition's first season, Villa have failed to live up to their promise in recent seasons and suffered double Wembley heartbreak in 2010, losing in both the FA Cup semi-finals and the League Cup Final.

Founded: 1874   **Ground:** Villa Park
Capacity: 42,780   **Nickname:** Villans

HONOURS

League Champions: 1894, 1896, 1897, 1899, 1900, 1910, 1981
FA Cup: 1887, 1895, 1897, 1905, 1913, 1920, 1957
League Cup: 1961, 1975, 1977, 1994, 1996
European Cup: 1982
European Super Cup: 1983
Charity Shield: 1981

ASTON VILLA

Gabby Agbonlahor

Frank Lampard

Founded: 1905   **Ground:** Stamford Bridge
Capacity: 41,840   **Nickname:** Blues/Pensioners

HONOURS

League Champions: 1955, 2005, 2006, 2010
Division Two: 1984, 1989
FA Cup: 1970, 1997, 2000, 2007, 2009, 2010, 2012
League Cup: 1965, 1998, 2005, 2007
Community Shield: 1955, 2000, 2005, 2009
Champions League: 2012
Cup Winners' Cup: 1971, 1998
UEFA Super Cup: 1998

Three-times Premier League winners Chelsea underwent a massive transformation when Russian oil billionaire Roman Abramovich took over the club in 2003. The Blues were able to buy in some top-class players and pay massive salaries just months after fears over their existence. The arrival of Portuguese boss Jose Mourinho was also another major step forward and resulted in consecutive titles in 2005 and 2006. They won their third Premier League in 2010, as well as the FA Cup, during Carlo Ancelotti's first season in charge. Their greatest-ever moment came when they lifted the European Cup in May 2012 with victory over Bayern Munich.

PLAYERS

MOST APPEARANCES:
Ron Harris (1961-80) 795
Premier League: Frank Lampard (2001-)
Midfielder Lampard is just a handful of league appearances ahead of his captain and friend John Terry. The two England men have been stalwarts for both club and country but it's Lampard's incredible goal-scoring record from midfield that has made him "Super Frank" with the Blues faithful.

MOST GOALS:
Bobby Tambling (1959-70) 202
Premier League: Frank Lampard
Lampard is the most free-scoring midfielder in the Premier League. He has twice hit four goals in single matches for the Blues – impressive for a striker, amazing by a midfielder. Lampard's knack of bursting forward from midfield and then unleashing tremendous thunderbolt shots have made him a lethal weapon.

FAN FAVOURITE:
Didier Drogba
Twenty-nine Premier League goals in 2009-10 gave Drogba the Golden Boot. He is one of the strongest, most lethal finisher around and if he hadn't been struck down by injuries his total could have been much higher. Capable of holding the ball up, going past defenders or taking deadly and accurate free-kicks, the Ivory Coast ace has been vital for the Blues. Hit their European Cup winner in 2012 before his departure from Stamford Bridge.

Didier Drogba

CHELSEA

Everton

PLAYERS

MOST APPEARANCES:
Neville Southall (1981-98) 751
Premier League: David Unsworth (1991-97, 98-04) 302

Two spells at Goodison Park, mostly during the Premier League years, saw him rated by fans as a tough, reliable defender. Twenty penalties from his first 23 spot-kicks for the team saw him set a new club record in 2002, an even more remarkable feat for a player used as a central defender or full back.

MOST GOALS:
Dixie Dean (1925-37) 383
Premier League: Tim Cahill (2004-12)

The £2m spent on taking midfielder Cahill to Goodison from Millwall in 2004 is arguably one of the best bits of transfer business Everton have ever conducted. A typical Aussie who doesn't know the meaning of being beaten, Cahill has won his midfield battles and scored some brilliant and vital goals for Everton. He was also the first Aussie to score in a World Cup Finals.

Tim Cahill

FAN FAVOURITE:
Nikica Jelavic

Having signed on from Rangers for £5m in January 2012, the Croatia striker had a lot of prove. He did that instantly with 11 goals in his first 16 games for the Goodison Park side. The Toffees have been screaming out for a regular goal scorer for years and it could be that they have found just that man.

Founder members of the Football League and an ever-present in the Premier League since it began, Everton have a proud tradition. It's just a short walk across Stanley Park between Liverpool and Everton football clubs but the gulf between the pair has quite often been immense, particularly in terms of title-wins, although both have yet to win the Premier League. But when it comes to derby games between the two teams it's often hard to tell which side is the most highly rated. Ironically, Liverpool were formed by a group that broke away from Everton – who used to play at Anfield, their biggest rivals' ground! The Toffees have talked about moving to a brand new, bigger ground but have hit a number of planning and financial problems over the past few years.

Founded: 1878   **Ground:** Goodison Park
Capacity: 40,150   **Nickname:** Toffees

HONOURS

League Champions: 1891, 1915, 1928, 1932, 1939, 1963, 1970, 1985,1987
Division Two: 1931
FA Cup: 1906 1933, 1966, 1984, 1995
European Cup Winners' Cup: 1985
Charity Shield: 1928, 1932, 1963, 1970, 1984, 1985, 1986 (shared), 1987, 1995

Nikica Jelavic

Brian McBride

Founded: 1879   **Ground:** Craven Cottage
Capacity: 25,700   **Nickname:** Cottagers

HONOURS

Division One: 2001
Division Two: 1949, 1999
Division Three (South): 1932

Fulham are the oldest of the capital's top-flight clubs and one steeped in a lot of history, even if they are regarded as a smaller side. Under the ownership of wealthy Harrods boss Mohamed Al-Fayed they rose three divisions to the Premier League where they have remained since 2001. Roy Hodgson, now England boss, guided the Cottagers to one of their finest campaigns in 2009-10 when they reached the Europa League Final only to lose to Atletico Madrid in extra-time.

PLAYERS

MOST APPEARANCES:
Johnny Haynes (1952-70) 658
Premier League star:
Aaron Hughes (2007-)
The vital experience of the central defender was crucial to Fulham's progress in recent years. Calm, assured and consistent, Hughes has also played for both Newcastle United and Aston Villa and has captained Northern Ireland.

MOST GOALS:
Gordon Davies (1978-91) 178
Premier League star:
Brian McBride (2004-08) 33
The Cottagers renamed a bar after USA international striker McBride, their former club captain McBride notched more than 150 league appearances and 40 goals for Fulham where he won over the fans with his hard work and determination.

FAN FAVOURITE:
Clint Dempsey
The first Fulham player to hit double-figures of goals in a Premier League season, the USA international can play wide, just behind a frontman or as an out and out striker. He's now overtaken fellow countryman McBride as the highest scoring American in the English top-flight with 50 goals in his 184 games up to the end of 2011-12. Joined the Cottagers from New England Revolution in 2007 for around £2m, the highest fee then paid by a Premier League club for a player from the MLS.

FULHAM

Clint Dempsey

PLAYERS

MOST APPEARANCES:
Ian Callaghan (1960-78) 857
Premier League star:
Jamie Carragher (1996-)
The one-club defender is set to make his 700th appearance for his home-town club in 2012-13. Despite being an Everton fan as a boy, Carra has remained totally loyal to the Reds since 1996 and is likely to finish his career at Anfield.

MOST GOALS:
Ian Rush (1980-87, 88-96) 346
Premier League star:
Fernando Torres (2007-10) 65
The critics who wondered if the Spain striker could hack it in the Premier League have had their doubts shoved firmly down their throats. Despite injury problems he found the back of the net 81 times in 142 games. Sold to Chelsea for £50m in January 2010, giving the Reds a £30m profit.

FAN FAVOURITE:
Steven Gerrard
Playing for the team he supported from the Kop as a boy means Gerrard is living the dream. Like his big friend Carragher, Gerrard is a one-club player and at the end of season 2011-12 had reached the 577 game mark for the Anfield side, notching 149 goals in the process.

Steven Gerrard

With 18 league titles in the bag, at the end of the 2009-10 season Liverpool were still joint top in the league-winning stakes with Man United – but lost that record as their rivals clinched a 19th crown. Although they can boast FIVE European Cups, the Reds are still seeking that first, elusive Premier League title. Without doubt THE team of the 1970s and 80s, Liverpool have had cup success in the new millennium but not the league victory they crave so much.

Founded: 1892   **Ground:** Anfield
Capacity: 45,200   **Nickname:** Reds

HONOURS

League Champions: 1901, 1906, 1922, 1923, 1947, 1964, 1966, 1973, 1976, 1977, 1979, 1980, 1982, 1983, 1984, 1986, 1988, 1990
FA Cup: 1965, 1974, 1986, 1989, 1992, 2001, 2006
League Cup: 1981, 1982, 1983, 1984, 1995, 2001, 2003, 2012
European Cup: 1977, 1978, 1981, 1984, 2005
UEFA Cup: 1973, 1976, 2001
European Super Cup: 1977, 2001, 2005
Charity Shield: 1964*, 1965*, 1966, 1974, 1976, 1977*, 1979, 1980, 1982, 1986*, 1988, 1989, 1990*, 2001, 2006 (*shared)
Division Two: 1894, 1896, 1905, 1962

Jamie Carragher

LIVERPOOL

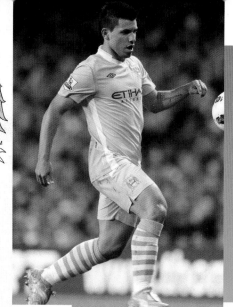
Sergio Aguero

MANCHESTER CITY

Founded: 1880   **Ground:** Etihad Stadium
Capacity: 47,800   **Nickname:** Citizens, Blues

HONOURS

League Champions: 1937, 1968, 2012
Division One: 2002
Division Two play-off winners: 1999
Division Two: 1899, 1903, 1910, 1928, 1947, 1966
FA Cup: 1904, 1934, 1956, 1969, 2011
League Cup: 1970, 1976
European Cup Winners' Cup: 1970
Charity Shield: 1937, 1968, 1972

PLAYERS

MOST CLUB APPEARANCES:
Alan Oakes (1959-76) 676
Premier League star: Joe Hart (2006-)
The England keeper has established himself as No.1 at City over the past few years, even pushing Republic of Ireland star Shay Given out of the keeper's spot – and that's no mean feat. Hart began his career at Shrewsbury and had loans at Tranmere, Blackpool and Birmingham City before sealing his spot at the Etihad Stadium.

MOST CLUB GOALS:
Eric Brook (1928-39) 176
Premier League star:
Shaun Goater (1998-03)
Six seasons with City, two in the Premier League, raised The Goat to legendary status. More than 100 goals in four of those season, and top scorer for the club each of those years, made him a hero. Fifty-two games and 13 Premiership goals may not sound great but his all-round contribution means he will never be forgotten.

FAN FAVOURITE:
Sergio Aguero
City thought he was good when they forked out a massive £38m to Atletico Madrid for the striker – and having bagged the goal that sealed their first Premier League title they can have no complaints. But the Argentina star has proved that he was one of their best buys ever with his clever movement, pace and lethal finishing that brought 30 goals in 48 game during his first season for the Citizens.

The whole world now knows about mega-rich Manchester City and their expensively assembled squad of superstars. But it wasn't that long ago that City nestled in the third tier of English football! Founder members of the Premiership, they were relegated in 1996 and dropped down another division in 1998, only to be promoted at the first attempt. They arrived back in the Premier League in 2000 for another season before suffering another relegation. Promoted back to the top-flight in 2002 City lifted their first Premier League crown in 2011-12.

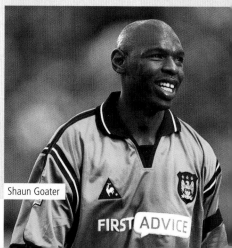
Shaun Goater

FIRST ADVICE

MANCHESTER UNITED

PLAYERS

MOST APPEARANCES:
Ryan Giggs 900+ (1991-)
Premier League star: Ryan Giggs
The likes of Giggsy will probably never be seen again. He started at the club as a trainee, has played for them all of his career and even retired from international football with Wales to prolong his club outings. Giggs had played 53 games for United before the Premier League began in 1992-93. He hit a new record of club appearances for the Red Devils in 2008, beating Bobby Charlton's previous best.

MOST GOALS:
Bobby Charlton (1956-73) 249
Premier League star: Paul Scholes (1994-)
There's very little between Scholes and Giggs in the goalscoring stakes with both over the 150 mark for United. That's an amazing achievement by two midfielders, with both of them cracking the 100 Premier League goal mark. Scholes retired in May 2011 only to return to action in January 2012.

FAN FAVOURITE:
Wayne Rooney
He cost them an initial £25m and at today's transfer prices that now looks a bargain. Rooney is another player set to pass the 150-goal mark for United having already notched more than 443 appearances and 198 goals for Everton and Man United at the end of season 2011-12.

Paul Scholes

The Premier League's most successful team with the division's most successful manager in Sir Alex Ferguson. Everyone else is still playing catch up with a side that are also officially one of the three biggest football teams in the world. They won the first Premier League in 1993 and 11 more titles followed to the end of 2011-12. Fergie ended the club's 26-year wait for English football's top trophy. Incredibly, back in 1974 United were relegated to the second tier but bounced back at the first attempt.

Founded: 1878   **Ground:** Old Trafford
Capacity: 76,000   **Nickname:** Red Devils

HONOURS

League Champions: 1908, 1911, 1952, 1956, 1957, 1965, 1967, 1993, 1994, 1996, 1997, 1999, 2000, 2001, 2003, 2007, 2008, 2009, 2011
Division Two: 1936, 1975
FA Cup: 1909, 1948, 1963, 1977, 1983, 1985, 1990, 1994, 1996, 1999, 2004
League Cup: 1992, 2006, 2009, 2010
Charity/Community Shield: 1908, 1911, 1952, 1956, 1957, 1965*, 1967*, 1977*, 1983, 1990*, 1993, 1994, 1996, 1997, 2003, 2007, 2008, 2010, 2011 (*shared)
European Cup: 1968, 1999, 2008
UEFA Cup Winners' Cup: 1991
UEFA Super Cup: 1991
Intercontinental Cup: 1999
Club World Cup: 2008

Wayne Rooney

NEWCASTLE UNITED

Alan Shearer

Founded: 1892 **Ground:** St. James' Park
Capacity: 52,300 **Nickname:** Magpies/Toon

HONOURS

League Champions: 1905, 1907, 1909, 1927
Second-First Division/Championship:
1965, 1993, 2010
FA Cup: 1910, 1924, 1932, 1951, 1952, 1955
Community Shield: 1909
Inter Cities Fairs Cup: 1969

The fans pack into St. James' Park for every home game but they have had little to cheer in recent years except their amazing return to the Premier League in 2010 as Championship champions after just one season away. Their heady Premier League days under Kevin Keegan, Kenny Dalglish and Sir Bobby Robson when they challenged for the title and were regular competitors in Europe appeared light years away until Alan Pardew took them to fifth in the Premier League in 2012.

PLAYERS

MOST APPEARANCES:
Jimmy Lawrence (1904-22) 496
Premier League: Shay Given (1997-09)
With 354 league appearances under his belt Given is among Newcastle's most loyal servants. Even his move to Manchester City didn't dim the Geordies' view of a player they knew had given his all for the Toon during an impressive run between the sticks. His quality saves and performances undoubtedly earned Newcastle vital points and made Given one of the most highly rated keepers in the top-flight.

MOST GOALS:
Alan Shearer (1996-06) 206
Premier League: Alan Shearer
Quite simply, it is highly unlikely that any player is ever going to match the goal scoring prowess of Big Al. If anyone does… they are assured of God-like status on Tyneside. Shearer is the Premier League's all-time top goalscorer, another record that he is unlikely to lose. Deadly with either foot and his head, the legendary No.9 could also hold the ball up like no other centre-forward. Sheer class.

FAN FAVOURITE:
Fabricio Coloccini
As a £10m arrival from Deportivo in 2008 much was expected of the Argentina defender. But his early days at Newcastle were not his best – then he progressed into being one of the Premier League's best centre halves, stayed with the club when they were relegated for a season and was then handed the captain's armband. Voted into the PFA Team of the Season for 2011-12.

Fabricio Coloccini

NORWICH CITY

MOST APPEARANCES:
Ron Ashman (1947-63) 662
Premier League: Mark Bowen (1987-96)
The Wales defender made 119 Premier League appearances for the Canaries during the first three years of the competition and stayed at Carrow Road when they were relegated. He was voted the club's best-ever left back and is in their Hall of Fame.

MOST GOALS:
Johnny Gavin (1948-54) 132
Premier League: Chris Sutton (1991-94)
The striker was with the Canaries when the Premier League began and in their first two seasons in the competition he hit 33 goals, 25 of them in his second year, which earned him a move to Blackburn.

FAN FAVOURITE:
Adam Drury
It would be easy to plump for keeper John Ruddy or striker Grant Holt but defender Drury saw it all during his time at Carrow Road. City's Player of the Year in 2003 suffered relegations and enjoyed promotions and was the strong, committed team player that every side would love to have. Left in summer 2012.

Chris Sutton

Adam Drury

Norwich finished third in the first-ever Premier League in 1992-93 but in 1995 they were relegated. At the end of 2003-04 they bounced back to the top-flight for just one season. They spent three seasons in the Championship before dropping to the third tier of English football for one season, then winning League One in 2010. The Canaries won their second consecutive promotion in 2011, returning to the Premier League as Championship runners-up.

Founded: 1902   **Ground:** Carrow Road
Capacity: 27,000   **Nickname:** Canaries, Yellows

HONOURS

League One: 2010
First Division: 2004
Division Two: 1972, 1986
Division Three: 1934
League Cup: 1962, 1985

QUEENS PARK RANGERS

Adel Taarabt

Founded: 1882   **Ground:** Loftus Road
Capacity: 18,300   **Nickname:** Hoops, Rangers, Rs

HONOURS

Championship: 2011
Division Two: 1983
Division Three: 1948, 1967
League Cup: 1967

QPR were founder members of the Premier League but were relegated at the end of 1995-96 after selling leading goalscorer Les Ferdinand. They suffered a further relegation to the third tier before returning to the second-flight in 2004. They remained in the Championship until 2011 despite takeovers, which included being bought out by F1 racing bosses Bernie Ecclestone and Flavio Briatore in 2007 - plus battles against financial problems. Neil Warnock was brought in to get them promoted, which he did, as champions.

PLAYERS

MOST APPEARANCES:
Tony Ingham (1950-63) 548
Premier League star:
Andy Impey 142 (1990-97)
Impey was three times QPR's Player of the Season in their first three Premier League years operating at left back or on the wing. He was plucked from non league Yeading in West London and made his first team debut at the age of 18.

MOST GOALS:
George Goddard (1926-33) 186
Premier League star:
Les Ferdinand 60 (1987-95)
The £6m club record sale of Ferdinand to Newcastle signalled the start of bad times for Rangers. The striker they had plucked from non-league Hayes for £30,000 hit double-figures in goals each of his three Premier League seasons at Loftus Road.

FAN FAVOURITE:
Adel Taarabt
After two loan spells, the Morocco midfielder finally joined QPR from Tottenham in 2010 for a bargain £1m. Talented but unpredictable he's the type of player who can influence the outcome of a game with his trickery. Always likely to move on as managers battled to harness his skills.

Les Ferdinand

PLAYERS

MOST APPEARANCES:
Martin Hicks (1978-91) 603
Premier League star:
Marcus Hahnemann (2002-09) 76
The USA keeper was an ever-present during Reading's first appearance in the Premier League having played a key part in their rise from the Championship. He kept 13 clean sheets in the first year and despite relegation was one of the best shot-stopper in the division in their second season.

MOST LEAGUE GOALS:
Trevor Senior (1983-87, 88-92) 184
Premier League star:
Kevin Doyle (2005-09)
Thirteen goals in his first Premier League season despite injury and six in his second when the Royals were relegated hide the fact that the Republic of Ireland star contributed far more than goals to the side. Made a total of 164 appearances for Reading and scored 56 goals.

FAN FAVOURITE:
Ian Harte
The veteran Republic of Ireland defender proved that class is permanent by playing a vital role in the Royals' return to the Premier League in 2012. A snip at £100,000 from Carlisle, the former Leeds United star not only defends but is also deadly at free-kicks.

Kevin Doyle

Ian Harte

Founder members of Division Three in 1920, Reading suffered financial problems in the 1980s and almost merged with Oxford United. But the arrival of local millionaire businessman John Madejski in 1990 changed their fortunes. He built them a new ground and kept his promise of getting them to the Premier League in 2006, thanks to a record Championship points tally. They were relegated in 2008 but bounced back to the top-flight as Championship champions in 2012 with Brian McDermott as manager.

Founded: 1871   **Ground:** Madejski Stadium
Capacity: 24,160   **Nickname:** Royals

HONOURS
Championship: 2006, 2012
Division Two: 1994
Third Division: 1926, 1986
Fourth Division: 1979
Full Members Cup: 1988

READING

SOUTHAMPTON

Adam Lallana

Founded: 1885   **Ground:** St. Mary's
Capacity: 32,690   **Nickname:** Saints

HONOURS

Division Three: 1960
FA Cup: 1976
Football League Trophy: 2010

Saints moved from their famous Dell ground to St. Mary's in 2001. They were founder members of the Premier League but were relegated to the Championship in 2005, they dropped into League One in 2009. A ten-point deduction imposed when the club went into administration all but sealed their relegation. Promoted back to the Championship as League One runners-up in 2011, they returned to the Premier League in 2012, as second in the Championship.

PLAYERS

MOST APPEARANCES:
Terry Paine (1956-74) 809
Premier League star:
Matt Oakley (1994-06) 232
The midfielder began his career with the club and spent more than a decade as a first-team regular, playing 30 games or more in seven seasons. Played a total of 261 league games for the club.

MOST GOALS:
Mick Channon (1966-77, 79-82) 227
Premier League star:
Matt Le Tissier (1986-02)
Channon scored 185 league goals in his 227 total, Le Tiss hit 162 for the club, 210 in total. Known as Le God, the Guernsey-born one-club midfielder won just eight England caps. Missed just one of 48 penalties taken.

FAN FAVOURITE:
Adam Lallana
Although keeper Kelvin Davis has now clocked more than 240 appearances for the Saints over six years, it's home grown Lallana who has been fans' biggest hero as they have battle back to the top-flight. They thought they would lose the midfielder but he stuck with the side he joined at the age of 12 in 2000.

Matt Le Tissier

PLAYERS

MOST CLUB APPEARANCES:
John McCue (1946-60) 675
Premier League star: Rory Delap (2008-)
Noted for his long-throws, Delap is much more than a lobber of the ball! The much-travelled Irish midfielder has been an important contributor to the Potters' success over the past three seasons and has rarely missed a game.

MOST GOALS:
John Ritchie (1962-66, 69-75) 171
Premier League star:
Matt Etherington (2009-)
The lively winger has rediscovered his form during his time with Stoke, winning player awards, scoring goals and creating chances for his team-mates. His form made him a fans' favourite and created calls for an England chance.

FAN FAVOURITE:
Ryan Shawcross (2007-)
The former Man United defender has grown in stature since joining Stoke and pushed himself into England reckoning. Sir Alex Ferguson was so reluctant to let him leave Old Trafford that he agreed a first-option buy-back clause. Solid and commanding, big things are expected of the player.

Matt Etherington

Many managers had tried and failed to get Stoke back in the top-flight after a 25-year absence but Tony Pulis pulled off the feat on the final day of the 2007-08 season. He achieved success in just two seasons making the Potters the oldest club to play in the Premier League. Pulis had been sacked by the club in 2005 and took over Plymouth for a year. He was brought back to the Britannia Stadium when the club had a change of ownership.

Founded: 1863   **Ground:** Britannia Stadium
Capacity: 27,700   **Nickname:** Potters

HONOURS

**Automatic promotion
to Premier League:** 2008
Division Two: 1933, 1963, 1993
Division Two play-off winners: 2002
Division Three (North): 1927
League Cup: 1972
Auto Windscreen Shield: 2000
Autoglass Trophy: 1992

Ryan Shawcross

STOKE CITY

SUNDERLAND

James McClean

Founded: 1879   **Ground:** Stadium of Light
Capacity: 49,000   **Nickname:** Black Cats

HONOURS
League Champions: 1892, 1893, 1895, 1902, 1913, 1936.
Championship: 2005, 2007
Second division: 1976
First division: 1996, 1999
Third division: 1988
FA Cup: 1937, 1973   **Charity Shield:** 1936

PLAYERS

MOST APPEARANCES:
Jim Montgomery, (1960-77) 627
Premier League star:
Niall Quinn (1996-02) 129
Although four other players – including Kevin Phillips – have currently made more Premier League appearances for the club, Quinn is still a legend on Wearside. The Republic of Ireland striker scored 69 goals and played a total of 220 games for the club and then donated around £1m from his testimonial game to charity.

MOST GOALS:
Bob Gurney (1925-50) 228
Premier League star:
Kevin Phillips (1997-03) 61
Premier League top scorer in 1999-2000 with 30 goals for the Black Cats, 'Super Kev' was also European Golden Boot winner that season. Fourteen strikes the following season helped towards his legendary status. Totalled 115 goals in 209 Premier and Division One games for the club.

FAN FAVOURITE:
James McClean
Signed from Derry at the aged of 21 for just £350,000 in August 2011, the midfielder made a massive impact in his first year at the Stadium of Light and has forced his way into the Republic of Ireland squad. Twenty-five appearances and six goals in a debut season is a great return – especially for a player the club had expected to play a bit part for 12 months!

Sunderland have moved between the top-flight and the second tier for a number of years. They won Division One in 1996 to get their first crack at the Premier League but after just one season were relegated. They lost the play-off final in 1998 but the following year won Division One and got back to the top-flight. In 2003 they were again relegated but two years later again won the second tier. After relegation in 2006, then Sunderland chairman Niall Quinn appointed Roy Keane as manager and he took the side from bottom to the title. He stayed one season in the Premier League before quitting.

Kevin Phillips

PLAYERS

MOST APPEARANCES:
Roger Freestone (1989-04) 699
Premier League: Scott Sinclair (2010-)
The winger played all 38 games during the Swans' debut season in the Premier League and City will be looking to tie him down to a new long term contract. The former England Under-21 star joined Swansea from Chelsea in August 2010 for a bargain £1m after spending time on loan with a number of clubs.

MOST LEAGUE GOALS:
Ivor Allchurch (1950-58, 65-68) 164
Premier League: Danny Graham (2011-)
The former Middlesbrough and Carlisle striker hit 12 Premier League goals in 36 appearances during 2011-12 having arrived from Watford a £3.5m deal in June 2011. He added two more goals in two FA Cup games.

FAN FAVOURITE:
Nathan Dyer
After a successful loan spell, Dyer from Southampton in 2009. The winger has been impressive since his move to South Wales. The Swans Supporters' Player of the Year in their play-off winning season of 2011. The 24-year-old played 34 times in the Premier League last season, scoring five goals.

Danny Graham

Nathan Dyer

Three promotions in four seasons between 1978 and 1981 saw Swansea rise from the fourth tier of English football to the top-flight. It was the first time in their history that they were in Division One, now the Premier League. By 1986 they were back in the old Division Four after suffering a number of financial problems. They were promoted to the Championship as League One Champions in 2008. They became the first Welsh side to play in the Premier League when they won the 2011 play-off final 4-2 against Reading, Sinclair scoring a hat-trick.

Founded: 1912   **Ground:** Liberty Stadium
Capacity: 20,530   **Nickname:** Swans, Jacks

HONOURS

Championship play-off final: 2011
League One: 2008
Third Division: 2000
Football League Trophy: 1994, 2006
Welsh Cup: 1913, 1932, 1950, 1961, 1966, 1981, 1982, 1983, 1989, 1991

SWANSEA CITY

TOTTENHAM

Gareth Bale

Founded: 1882   Ground: White Hart Lane
Capacity: 36,230   Nickname: Spurs

HONOURS

League Champions: 1951, 1961
Division Two: 1920, 1950
FA Cup: 1901, 1921, 1961, 1962, 1967, 1981, 1982, 1991
League Cup: 1971, 1973, 1999, 2008
Charity Shield: 1921, 1951, 1961, 1962, 1967*, 1981*, 1991* (*shared)
UEFA Cup: 1972, 1984
Cup Winners' Cup: 1963

Tottenham have been in the Premier League since it started although they did flirt with relegation in 2008. The arrival of boss Harry Redknapp saved them from the drop and in 2010 they qualified for the Champions League for the first time thanks to their highest-ever Premier League finish, fourth. In 1961, they became the first club in the 20th century to complete the League and FA Cup Double.

PLAYERS

MOST APPEARANCES:
Steve Perryman (1969-86) 854
Premier League star:
Darren Anderton (1992-04) 299
Mention Darren Anderton and many fans will smile knowingly at his nickname of 'Sicknote'. Yet the England midfielder was just one game short of making 300 Premier League appearances for Spurs. He scored 34 top-flight goals for the side – not bad for a player who missed plenty of matches with various problems!

MOST GOALS:
Jimmy Greaves (1961-70) 266
Premier League star:
Teddy Sheringham (1992-97, 01-03) 98
England striker Sheringham scored a total of 124 goals in 277 games for Spurs during two spells at White Hart Lane, punctuated by his time with Man United. Ninety-eight top-flight goals from 236 games is a great return for a player often used as a second striker. His fantastic link up skills and all round vision marked him down as the type of player Tottenham fans love.

FAN FAVOURITE:
Gareth Bale
The Wales star can play left back or left wing but he has also proved that he can torment the opposition when given a free role. Tottenham know they face a big challenge to keep hold of a player who only turned 23 in summer 2012 but Bale has pledged his allegiance to White Hart Lane. Joined Spurs from Southampton in 2007 for an initial £5m.

Teddy Sheringham

PLAYERS

MOST APPEARANCES:
Tony Brown (1963-81) 720
Premier League star:
Jonathan Greening (2004-10) 106
The former Man United and Middlesbrough battler was a vital cog in the Baggies midfield and endured a roller-coaster ride between the Premier League and Championship. He was often the club's star man but eventually moved to Fulham after a total of 106 Premier games, 224 in total.

MOST GOALS:
Tony Brown (1963-81) 279
Premier League star:
Peter Odemwingie (2010-)
The Nigeria striker joined the Baggies from Lokomotiv Moscow for what has proved to be a bargain £500,000. His first 60 Premier League appearances produced 25 goals, making him the club's most prolific scorer in the competition until the end of 2011-12. Three times Premier League Player of the Month in his first two seasons.

FAN FAVOURITE:
James Morrison
The former Middlesbrough midfielder, who can operate centrally or as a winger, arrived at the Hawthorns for just over £2m. Although he turned out for England at youth level up to Under-20 he has pledged his senior allegiance to Scotland. Morrison is a battler who has added vital goals to his repertoire.

Peter Odemwingie

West Brom made their Premier League bow under Gary Megson in 2002 but lasted just one season. After just one campaign in the second tier they were promoted again in 2005 – but in 2007 they went back down! Again, they were down for just one season and came back up as Champions. But Tony Mowbray's side again lasted just one campaign in the top-flight. After one more term in the Championship the Baggies were promoted as runners-up in 2010 under the guidance of Roberto Di Matteo. He was replaced by Roy Hodgson who brought stability to the club before taking over as England boss.

Founded: 1878   **Ground:** Hawthorns
Capacity: 26,270   **Nickname:** Baggies

HONOURS
League Champions: 1920
Division Two: 1902, 1911, 2008
Division Two play-off winners: 1993
FA Cup: 1888, 1892, 1931, 1954, 1968
League Cup: 1966
Charity Shield: 1920, 1954* (*shared)

James Morrison

WEST HAM UNITED

Paolo Di Canio

Founded: 1895　　**Ground:** Upton Park Boleyn Ground
Capacity: 35,000　　**Nickname:** Hammers

HONOURS
Championship play-off winners: 2005, 2012
Division Two: 1958, 1981
FA Cup: 1964, 1975, 1980
Charity Shield: 1964 (shared)
Cup Winners' Cup: 1965

West Ham competed in the second Premier League season in 1993 after gaining promotion from the old Division One - but were relegated in 2003 after a series of good finishes. They came up from the Championship at the second attempt, by winning the play-off final against Preston. They stayed up by just one place at the end of 2009-10 but went down the following season. They bounced back at the first attempt with a 2-1 play-off final victory over Blackpool. The club will forever be linked with England's 1966 World Cup win as they provided Bobby Moore, Geoff Hurst and Martin Peters for that side.

PLAYERS

MOST APPEARANCES:
Billy Bonds (1967-88) 793
Premier League star:
Robert Green (2006-12) 177
The keeper joined the Hammers from Norwich for £2m after more than 240 appearances for the Carrow Road side. Played every league game when the side dropped to the Championship for the season, including play-off semis and final. Moved to QPR on a free in summer 2012 after a total of 241 appearances for the Hammers.

MOST GOALS:
Vic Watson (1920-35) 326
Premier League star:
Paolo Di Canio 48 (1999-03)
Incredible skills endeared the Italian to the Hammers' faithful and during his time at Upton Park the eccentric striker hit the headlines for good and bad reasons. He won a fair play award, scored amazing goals but was also in trouble with officials. Hit 48 Premier League goals in 118 games, totalling 52 in 141 matches. Carlton Cole is set to beat that top-flight total for the club.

FAN FAVOURITE:
Mark Noble
Locally born midfielder Noble joined the club whilst still at school and up to the end of 2011-12 was their longest-serving player at the age of 25. Now has more than 200 games under his belt for the Hammers and played 20 times for England Under-21s.

Mark Noble

MOST LEAGUE APPEARANCES:
Kevin Langley (1981-86, 90-94) 317
Premier League star:
Emmerson Boyce (2006-)
With more than 170 appearances for the Latics – over 150 in the Premier League – the defender is an unsung hero for Wigan. The Barbados international arrived at the DW Stadium from Crystal Palace for just £1m.

MOST LEAGUE GOALS:
Andy Liddell (1998-03) 70
Premier League star:
Hugo Rodallega (2009-12) 24
Wigan haven't been a team noted for strikers and the 24-goal total that Rodallega had achieved by the end of season 2011-12 to become their highest-scorer in the top-flight highlights that fact. The Colombian was signed from Necaxa for £4.5m but after just two goals all campaign was released in summer 2012.

FAN FAVOURITE:
Shaun Maloney
Signed from Celtic for just under £1m in summer 2011, Scotland midfielder Maloney, then 28, proved to be an inspired buy. The former Scotland Player of the Year gives the Latics strength and guile in the centre of the park and dead ball options.

Hugo Rodallega

Shaun Maloney

Wigan reached the top-flight of English football for the first time ever in 2005 – and have stayed in the Premier League against all odds. Just ten years earlier they were in the old Division Three and completed their remarkable rise to the top after being taken over by sports clothing firm boss Dave Whelan. Paul Jewell was the manager who guided them from third tier to top, their automatic promotion to the Premier League confirmed on the final day of the 2003-04 season with a home win. A remarkable record for a team that only entered the League in 1978.

Founded: 1932   **Ground:** DW Stadium
Capacity: 25,100   **Nickname:** Latics

HONOURS

Division Two Champions: 2003
Division Three Champions: 1997
League Trophy: 1985, 1999

WIGAN ATHLETIC

THE PREMIER LEAGUE

The Premiership – or the Premier League as it is now known – kicked-off for the first time in season 1992-93.

There were 22 founding members, which included Leeds United, the reigning Division One champions.

The Elland Road side had lifted the top-flight trophy under boss Howard Wilkinson – still the last Englishman to win England's title.

Luton Town, Notts County and West Ham United missed out on the chance of taking part in the new competition as they had been relegated from the old Division One.

Ipswich Town and Middlesbrough, who had been promoted from the old Second Division, along with Blackburn Rovers who won that division's play-off final, would also join the new competition.

The other founders were the rest of the teams from Division One, who had broken away from League Football and won a £300m-plus television deal from BSkyB (now Sky) and the BBC.

Brian Deane scored the Premiership's first-ever goal as Manchester United lost 2-1 to Sheffield United on opening day.

But with Eric Cantona signing from Leeds United that November the Red Devils bounced back to win the first-ever Premier League and their eighth league title.

2001-02

ALL THE WINNERS...

1992-93	Manchester United
1993-94	Manchester United
1994-95	Blackburn Rovers
1995-96	Manchester United
1996-97	Manchester United
1997-98	Arsenal
1998-99	Manchester United
199-00	Manchester United
2000-01	Manchester United
2001-02	Arsenal
2002-03	Manchester United
2003-04	Arsenal
2004-05	Chelsea
2005-06	Chelsea
2006-07	Manchester United
2007-08	Manchester United
2008-09	Manchester United
2009-10	Chelsea
2010-11	Manchester United
2011-12	Manchester City

ENGLAND'S TOP TIER PRE-1992
FOOTBALL LEAGUE 1888-1892

1889	Preston North End
1890	Preston North End
1891	Everton
1892	Sunderland

DIVISION ONE 1893-1992

1893	Sunderland
1894	Aston Villa
1895	Sunderland
1896	Aston Villa
1897	Aston Villa
1898	Sheffield United
1899	Aston Villa
1900	Aston Villa
1901	Liverpool
1902	Sunderland
1903	The Wednesday

1904	The Wednesday	**1953**	Arsenal
1905	Newcastle United	**1954**	Wolverhampton Wanderers
1906	Liverpool	**1955**	Chelsea
1907	Newcastle United	**1956**	Manchester United
1908	Manchester United	**1957**	Manchester United
1909	Newcastle United	**1958**	Wolverhampton Wanderers
1910	Aston Villa	**1959**	Wolverhampton Wanderers
1911	Manchester United	**1960**	Burnley
1912	Blackburn Rovers	**1961**	Tottenham
1913	Sunderland	**1962**	Ipswich Town
1914	Blackburn Rovers	**1963**	Everton
1915	Everton	**1964**	Liverpool
1916-1919	World War I	**1965**	Manchester United
1920	West Bromwich Albion	**1966**	Liverpool
1921	Burnley	**1967**	Manchester United
1922	Liverpool	**1968**	Manchester City
1923	Liverpool	**1969**	Leeds United
1924	Huddersfield Town	**1970**	Everton
1925	Huddersfield Town	**1971**	Arsenal
1926	Huddersfield Town	**1972**	Derby County
1927	Newcastle United	**1973**	Liverpool
1928	Everton	**1974**	Leeds United
1929	Sheffield Wednesday	**1975**	Derby County
1930	Sheffield Wednesday	**1976**	Liverpool
1931	Arsenal	**1977**	Liverpool
1932	Everton	**1978**	Nottingham Forest
1933	Arsenal	**1979**	Liverpool
1934	Arsenal	**1980**	Liverpool
1935	Arsenal	**1981**	Aston Villa
1936	Sunderland	**1982**	Liverpool
1937	Manchester City	**1983**	Liverpool
1938	Arsenal	**1984**	Liverpool
1939	Everton	**1985**	Everton
1940-46	World War II	**1986**	Liverpool
1947	Liverpool	**1987**	Everton
1948	Arsenal	**1988**	Liverpool
1949	Portsmouth	**1989**	Arsenal
1950	Portsmouth	**1990**	Liverpool
1951	Tottenham	**1991**	Arsenal
1952	Manchester United	**1992**	Leeds United

BARNSLEY

PLAYERS

MOST LEAGUE APPEARANCES: Barry Murphy (1962-78) 514
MOST GOALS: Ernie Hine (1921-26,34-38) 150

Division One runners-up in 1997, Barnsley then enjoyed their one and only season in England's top-flight. They were victims of the biggest away win of the season when Chelsea thumped them 6-0 at Oakwell but made their mark that term by dumping Man United out of the FA Cup. Former Reds player Danny Wilson took the side up but as the side struggled in the top-flight he departed for rivals Sheffield Wednesday. Barnsley finished second bottom, six points away from safety and with the league's worst goal difference, minus 45.

Founded: 1887
Ground: Oakwell
Capacity: 23,000
Nickname: Reds/Tykes

HONOURS

Promotion to Premier League: 1997
Promotion to Championship via play-off final: 2006

BIRMINGHAM CITY

PLAYERS

MOST APPEARANCES: Gil Merrick (1939-60) 713
MOST GOALS: Joe Bradford (1920-35) 267

After losing three consecutive play-off semi-finals, Birmingham City finally reached the Premier League in 2002 under the guidance of boss Steve Bruce. It was their first appearance in the top-flight for 16 years. After three seasons they were relegated, only to bounce back at the first attempt as Championship runners-up. One season later, following the departure of Bruce, they were down again but returned as runners-up under Alex McLeish. They were relegated again in 2010-11 and failed to come back up through the play-offs.

Founded: 1875
Ground: St. Andrews
Capacity: 30,000
Nickname: Blues

HONOURS

Division Two: 1893, 1921, 1948, 1955
Championship play-off winners: 2002
Second Division: 1995
League Cup: 1963

BLACKBURN ROVERS

PLAYERS

MOST APPEARANCES: Derek Fazackerley (1969-87) 671
MOST GOALS: Simon Garner (1978-92) 194

Blackburn will forever be remembered as the second team to win the Premier League – and the only team to have won that title and be relegated! Rovers spent a fortune on players like Alan Shearer and took the title in 1995 under boss Kenny Dalglish. In 1999 they were relegated from the top-flight but in 2001 were promoted as Championship runners-up under Graeme Souness. They were again relegated in 2011-12 when Steve Kean was in charge.

Founded: 1875
Ground: Ewood Park
Capacity: 31,300
Nickname: Rovers

HONOURS

League Champions: 1912, 1914, 1995 **Division Two:** 1939
Division Two play-off winners: 1992 **Division Three:** 1975 **FA Cup:** 1884, 1885, 1886, 1890, 1891,1928 **League Cup:** 2002
Full Members Cup: 1987

BLACKPOOL

PLAYERS

MOST APPEARANCES: Jimmy Armfield (1954-71) 627
MOST GOALS: Jimmy Hampson (1927-38) 252

Blackpool kicked off in the Premier League for the first time-ever in August 2010. But it was not their first time in England's top-flight. Having plummeted to the very bottom of the league ladder, the Tangerines arrived back at the summit for the first time in 39 years. They are the first club to be promoted through all four divisions via the play-off finals and were the 44th team to appear in the Premier League. They were relegated after one year and then beaten in the 2012 play-off final by West Ham.

Founded: 1887
Ground: Bloomfield Road
Capacity: 16,220
Nickname: Tangerines/Seasiders

HONOURS

Division Two: 1930
Championship play-off winners: 2010 **Division Three play-off winners:** 2001 **League One play-off winner** 2007 **Division Four play-off winners:** 1992 **FA Cup:** 1953 **League Trophy:** 2002, 2004

BOLTON

PLAYERS

MOST APPEARANCES: Eddie Hopkinson (1952-70) 578
MOST GOALS: Nat Lofthouse (1946-60) 285

Manager Bruce Rioch first guided Bolton into the Premier League via the play-offs in 1995. The Football League founding members were back in the top-flight after a 15-year absence that saw them plummet as low as Division Four (League Two). Colin Todd was boss as they went straight back down – to bounce back up immediately under the same gaffer! They again went down and failed in the play-off final. Sam Allardyce took them back to the Premier League in 2001 but they were relegated in 2012 under Owen Coyle.

Founded: 1874
Ground: Reebok Stadium
Capacity: 28,100
Nickname: Trotters

HONOURS
First division: 1997
Second division: 1909, 1978
Third division: 1973 **Division One play-off winners:** 1995, 2001 **FA Cup:** 1923, 1926, 1929, 1958 **Charity Shield:** 1958 **Football League Trophy:** 1989

BRIGHTON & HOVE ALBION

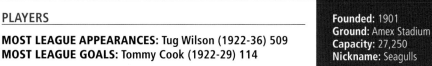

PLAYERS

MOST LEAGUE APPEARANCES: Tug Wilson (1922-36) 509
MOST LEAGUE GOALS: Tommy Cook (1922-29) 114

Brighton joined the Football League in 1920 and rose to the top-flight between 1979 and 1983. The late 1990s saw them almost lose their league status and suffer financial difficulties. They reached the Championship in 2004-05 although they only stayed there for two seasons. Following promotion as League One champions, the club moved to its new ground at Falmer for season 2011-12.

Founded: 1901
Ground: Amex Stadium
Capacity: 27,250
Nickname: Seagulls

HONOURS
League One: 2002, 2011
League One play-offs: 2004
League Two: 1965, 2001
Charity Shield: 1910

BRISTOL CITY

PLAYERS

MOST APPEARANCES: John Atyeo 645 (1951-66) 645
MOST GOALS: John Atyeo (1951-66) 351

Bristol City were runners-up in England's top-flight way back in 1907 when it was still known as Division One. The Robins came close to clinching a Premier League place when they reached the Championship play-off final in 2008. But the side, then managed by Gary Johnson, were beaten 1-0 by Hull City. Johnson, who had joined from Yeovil in 2005, had already won them promotion from League One during his second year in charge..

Founded: 1897
Ground: Ashton Gate
Capacity: 21,400
Nickname: Robins

HONOURS
Division 2 Champions, 1906 **Division 3 (South) Champions** 1923, 1927, 1955 **Freight Rover Trophy** 1986 **LDV Vans Trophy** 2003 **Welsh Cup** 1934

BURNLEY

PLAYERS

MOST LEAGUE APPEARANCES: Jerry Dawson (1907-28) 522
MOST LEAGUE GOALS: George Beel (1923-32) 178

Founder members of the Football League, Burnley were promoted to Division One in 2000 and when it became the Championship they looked a decent bet for promotion. But their form slumped until Owen Coyle took over as boss late in 2007. The following campaign, his first full season in charge, he took them to the play-off final where they beat Sheffield United 1-0 thanks to a Wade Elliott goal. Their first appearance in England's top-flight for 33 years lasted just one season, the Clarets being relegated after Coyle joined Bolton.

Founded: 1882
Ground: Turf Moor
Capacity: 22,500
Nickname: Clarets

HONOURS
Championship play-off winners: 2009 **Division One:** 1921, 1960 **Division Two:** 1898, 1973 **Division Three:** 1982 **Division Two play-off winners:** 1994 **Division Four:** 1992 **FA Cup:** 1914 **Charity Shield:** 1973, 1960 (shared)

PLAYERS

MOST APPEARANCES: Phil Dwyer (1972-85) 531
MOST GOALS: Len Davies (1920-31) 148

Cardiff are the only non-English team to have won the FA Cup, their victory coming against Arsenal in 1927. They were beaten finalists in 1925 and 2008. The Bluebirds have also played in all four divisions in England, but have not graced the top-flight since it was renamed Premier League. Robert Earnshaw is the only other player, besides record-holder Davies, to score more than 100 goals for City.

Founded: 1908
Ground: Cardiff City Stadium
Capacity: 26,800
Nickname: Bluebirds

HONOURS

FA Cup: 1927 **Charity Shield:** 1927 **Division 3 (South):** 1947 **Division Three:** 1993 **Welsh Cup:** 1912, 1920, 1922, 1923, 1927, 1928, 1930, 1956, 1959, 1964, 1965, 1967, 1968, 1969, 1970, 1971, 1973, 1974, 1976, 1988, 1992, 1993.

CARDIFF CITY

PLAYERS

MOST APPEARANCES: Sam Bartram (1934-56) 623
MOST GOALS: Derek Hales (1973-76, 78-85) 168

Charlton left their traditional home at the Valley between 1985 and 1992 and ground-share with Crystal Palace and then West Ham when they were hit by financial problems. After playing in the lower leagues for a number of years Charlton reached the Premier League via the play-offs for 1998-99. They were relegated after one season, bounced back and stayed until 2007 when they went down to the Championship and then into League One in 2009. They returned to the Championship in 2012 as League One Champions.

Founded: 1905
Ground: The Valley
Capacity: 27,100
Nickname: Addicks

HONOURS

League One: 2012
Division One: 2000
Division One play-offs: 1998
FA Cup: 1947

CHARLTON ATHLETIC

PLAYERS

MOST APPEARANCES: Jim Cannon (1973-88) 660
MOST GOALS: Peter Simpson (1930-36) 153

Palace were relegated at the end of the first Premier League season. Since then they have been promoted and relegated three times, enjoying just four seasons in the top-flight since 1993. The rest of the time they have spent in the second tier, although Palace did slump as low as the old Divisions Three and Four in their history. Financial problems have dogged them since the start of 2000s.

Founded: 1905
Ground: Selhurst Park
Capacity: 26,300
Nickname: Eagles

HONOURS

Division One: 1994
Division Two 1979
Second Division play-off winners: 1989,
First Division play-off winners: 1997, 2004
Full Members Cup: 1991

CRYSTAL PALACE

PLAYERS

MOST APPEARANCES: Kevin Hector (1966-78, 80-82) 589
MOST GOALS: Steve Bloomer (1892-06, 10-14) 332

Legendary manager Brian Clough led Derby to the top-flight title in 1972 and 1975, re-establishing them as a force in English football. The Rams are one of only ten clubs to have played in every season of the Football League since they were a founder member. They moved from the Baseball Ground to the purpose-built Pride Park in 1997. Clough's son Nigel took over as boss in 2009.

Founded: 1884
Ground: Pride Park
Capacity: 33,600
Nickname: Rams

HONOURS

League Champions: 1972, 1975
Division Two: 1912, 1915, 19, 1987
FA Cup: 1946
Charity Shield: 1975

DERBY COUNTY

HUDDERSFIELD TOWN

PLAYERS

MOST APPEARANCES: Billy Smith (1913-34) 574
MOST GOALS: George Brown (1921-29) 159

Just to prove cash problems are nothing new, Town went into liquidation in 1912. Not long afterwards they were attracting crowds to a staggering 47,000! Three times champions of England, Huddersfield have massive potential. One of their most famous sons was Denis Law, the Scotland striker sold to Manchester City in 1961. Returned to the second tier in 2012 after an 11-year absence.

Founded: 1908
Ground: Galpharm Stadium
Capacity: 24,500
Nickname: Terriers

HONOURS

League One play-off: 2012
League Champions: 1924, 1925, 1926 **Division Two Champions:** 1970
Division Three play-offs: 1995
Division Four: 1980
Division Flour play-offs: 2004
FA Cup: 1922
Charity Shield: 1922

HULL CITY

PLAYERS

MOST APPEARANCES: Andy Davidson (1952-68) 579
MOST GOALS: Chris Chilton (1960-71) 222

For a club that kicked off the new millennium by almost going bust, Hull City have made remarkable progress. At the end of 2002, they moved to the state of the art KC Stadium from their former home at Boothferry Park. And in May 2008 they made their first appearance at Wembley where they beat Bristol City in the play-off final to reach the top-flight of English football for the first time ever. They stayed in the Premier League for two seasons before relegation.

Founded: 1904
Ground: KC Stadium
Capacity: 25,500
Nickname: Tigers

HONOURS

Championship play-offs: 2008
Division Three: 1966

IPSWICH TOWN

PLAYERS

MOST APPEARANCES: Mick Mills 737 (1965-82) 737
MOST GOALS: Ray Crawford (1958-63, 65-68) 218

Ipswich's success in Europe, winning the league and being managed by former England bosses Sir Alf Ramsey and Sir Bobby Robson will forever by remembered. World Cup-winning gaffer Ramsey took the Blues to the League title in 1962. Sir Bobby led Town to FA Cup and UEFA Cup glory. Ipswich were founder members of the Premier League where they lasted for three years. They returned in 2000 but two seasons later were back in the Championship.

Founded: 1888
Ground: Portman Road
Capacity: 30,300
Nickname: Tractors Boys, Town, Blues

HONOURS

League Champions: 1962
Division One play-offs: 2000
Division Two: 1961, 1968, 1992
FA Cup: 1978
UEFA Cup: 1981

LEEDS UNITED

PLAYERS

MOST APPEARANCES: Jack Charlton 0(1952-73) 773
MOST GOALS: Peter Lorimer (1963-79) 238

The dramatic crash of Leeds United from the Premier League to League One stunned football. Once one of the giants of English football, and the last side to win the old First Division, they reached the semi-finals of the Champions League in 2001 before going into financial meltdown. They were relegated from the Premier League in 2004 and plunged to the third tier of English football for the first time in 2007. They returned to the Championship for 2010-11.

Founded: 1919
Ground: Elland Road
Capacity: 39,400
Nickname: Whites, United

HONOURS

League Champions: 1969, 1974, 1992 **Division Two:** 1924, 1964, 1990 **FA Cup:** 1972 **League Cup:** 1968
Charity Shield: 1969, 1992
Inter City Fairs Cup: 1968, 1971

LEICESTER CITY

PLAYERS

MOST APPEARANCES: Graham Cross (1960-76) 599
MOST GOALS: Arthur Chandler (1923-35) 273

Promoted to the Premier League via the play-off final in 1994, after two previous attempts failed, City lasted just one season. They were promoted at the first attempt, again through the play-offs, and stayed in the Premiership from 1996-02 when they were relegated for one season before gaining automatic promotion. One more season in the top-flight and they were back in the Championship, before a drop to League One for a season in 2008-09.

Founded: 1884
Ground: Walkers Stadium
Capacity: 32,200
Nickname: Foxes, City

HONOURS

Division Two: 1925, 1937, 1954, 1957, 1971, 1980
League One: 2009
Division One play-off winners: 1994, 1996
League Cup: 1964, 1997, 2000 **Charity Shield:** 1971

MIDDLESBROUGH

PLAYERS

MOST APPEARANCES: Tim Williamson (1902-1923) 602
MOST GOALS: George Camsell (1925-39) 345

Founding members of the Premier League in 1992, the Boro were relegated after one season. They were promoted in 1995, but stayed just two years, a points deduction sealing their fate. They returned at the first attempt but were relegated in 2009 after 11 consecutive seasons. Boro, who moved from their old Ayresome Park ground in 1995, survived massive financial problems in the 1980s and 2000s.

Founded: 1976
Ground: Riverside
Capacity: 34,900
Nickname: Boro, Smoggies

HONOURS

Division Two: 1927 1929, 1974, 1995
League Cup: 2004
Amateur Cup: 1895, 1898

MILLWALL

PLAYERS

MOST APPEARANCES: Barry Kitchener (1966-82) 602
MOST GOALS: Neil Harris (1998-04, 07-11) 138

Promotion in 1988 saw Millwall in the top-flight of English football for the first time-ever. They stayed for two seasons then suffered further relegations and financial difficulties. They missed out on a Premier League place, losing in the play-off semis in 2002 and then slumped to the third tier in 2006. The Lions lost out in the 2009 play-offs but gained automatic promotion to the Championship in 2010.

Founded: 1885
Ground: New Den
Capacity: 20,100
Nickname: Lions

HONOURS

League One play-offs: 2010
Division Two: 1988, 2001
Division Four: 1962

NOTTINGHAM FOREST

PLAYERS

MOST APPEARANCES: Bob McKinlay (1951-70) 692
MOST GOALS: Grenville Morris (1898-1913) 217

Forest fans will never forget the reign of Brian Clough who won them the league title, two European Cups and four League Cups. For a side of Forest's standing to win the League was great, to twice be Champions of Europe in two years was amazing. They were relegated after the Premier League's first season and Clough was sacked. They bounced back immediately but went back down in 1997. They once again came straight back, but again for one year. In 2005 they fell into the third tier, before returning to the Championship in 2008.

Founded: 1865
Ground: City Ground
Capacity: 30,600
Nickname: Forest, Tricky Trees,

HONOURS

League Champions: 1978
Division Two: 1907, 1922, 1998 **Division Three:** 1951
FA Cup: 1898, 1959
League Cup: 1978, 1979, 1989 1990 **Charity Shield:** 1978
European Cup: 1979, 1980
UEFA Super Cup: 1979

PETERBOROUGH UNITED

PLAYERS

MOST LEAGUE APPEARANCES: Tommy Robson (1968-81) 482
MOST LEAGUE GOALS: Jim Hall (1967-75) 122

Peterborough were elected to the Football League in 1960 and promoted as champions at the first attempt. They were relegated in 1968 for financial irregularities. Posh were in Division One between 1992 and 1994. Darren Ferguson led them to two successive promotions in 2008 and 2009, taking them to the Championship where they spent one season before relegation. They returned to the Championship with play-off final victory over Huddersfield in 2011.

Founded: 1934
Ground: London Road
Capacity: 14,600
Nickname: Posh

HONOURS

League One play-off: 2011
Third Division play-off: 1992
Third Division (4th tier) play-offs: 2000
Fourth Division: 1961, 1974

SHEFFIELD WEDNESDAY

PLAYERS

MOST APPEARANCES: Andrew Wilson (1900-20) 560
MOST GOALS: Andrew Wilson (1900-20) 217

Wednesday are a big club with a proud history and were founder members of the Premier League. Three appearances in the UEFA Cup (Europa League), the last in 1993, appeared a long way off following their relegation to League One in 2010. The Owls returned to the Championship as League One runners-up in 2011-12.

Founded: 1867
Ground: Hillsborough
Capacity: 39,700
Nickname: Owls

HONOURS

League champions: 1903, 1904, 1929, 1930
Division Two: 1900, 1926, 1952, 1956, 1959
League One play-offs: 2005 **FA Cup:** 1896, 1907, 1935 **League Cup:** 1991
Charity Shield: 1935

WATFORD

PLAYERS

MOST APPEARANCES: Luther Blissett (1976-92) 503
MOST GOALS: Luther Blissett (1976-92) 186

Under the management of former England boss Graham Taylor Watford completed a remarkable rise from Division Four to Division One between 1978 and 1982. Although they slipped out of the top-flight for a few years they arrived in the Premier League in 1999, again under Taylor, only to be relegated after one season. They bounced back for another season in 2006, when Aidy Boothroyd was in charge, and were then relegated back to the Championship.

Founded: 1881
Ground: Vicarage Road
Capacity: 17,400
Nickname: Hornets, Yellow Army

HONOURS

Championship play-off winners: 2006
Division Two play-off winners: 1999
Division Three: 1969, 1998
Division Four: 1978

WOLVERHAMPTON WANDERERS

PLAYERS

MOST APPEARANCES: Derek Parkin (1968-82) 609
MOST GOALS: Steve Bull (1986-99) 306

Wolves arrived in the Premier League via a play-off victory over Sheffield United in 2003 but went straight back down. They had failed in the play-offs just two years earlier but made no mistake the second time under manager Dave Jones. Promoted as Championship winners in 2009 under boss Mick McCarthy they avoided relegation until the end of 2011-12.

Founded: 1877
Ground: Molineux
Capacity: 31,500
Nickname: Wolves

HONOURS

League Champions: 1954, 1958, 1959 **Championship:** 2009
Second Division: 1932, 1977
First Division play-off: 2003
Third Division: 1989 **Fourth Division:** 1988 **FA Cup:** 1893, 1908, 1949, 1960 **League Cup:** 1974, 1980 **Charity Shield:** 1949*, 1954*, 1959, 1960* (*shared)

ENGLAND'S SECOND TIER

Currently known as The Championship, English football's second tier has also been called Division Two and Division One! From 1892 until the birth of the Premier League in 1992-93 it was Division Two, then it became Division One. It changed to The Championship in 2004.

2012

ALL THE WINNERS...

DIVISION TWO WINNERS 1893-1992

1893	Small Heath
1894	Liverpool
1895	Bury
1896	Liverpool
1897	Notts County
1898	Burnley
1899	Manchester City
1900	Sheffield Wednesday
1901	Grimsby Town
1902	West Bromwich Albion
1903	Manchester City
1904	Preston North End
1905	Liverpool
1906	Bristol City
1907	Nottingham Forest
1908	Manchester United
1909	Bolton Wanderers
1910	Manchester City
1911	West Bromwich Albion
1912	Derby County
1913	Preston North End
1914	Notts County
1915	Derby County
1915-19	World War I
1920	Tottenham
1921	Birmingham City
1922	Nottingham Forest
1923	Notts County
1924	Leeds United
1925	Leicester City
1926	Sheffield Wednesday
1927	Middlesbrough
1928	Manchester City
1929	Middlesbrough
1930	Blackpool
1931	Everton
1932	Wolverhampton Wanderers

1933	Stoke City		**1979**	Crystal Palace
1934	Grimsby Town		**1980**	Leicester City
1935	Brentford		**1981**	West Ham
1936	Manchester United		**1982**	Luton Town
1937	Leicester City		**1983**	Queens Park Rangers
1938	Aston Villa		**1984**	Chelsea
1939	Blackburn Rovers		**1985**	Oxford United
1939-46	World War II		**1986**	Norwich City
1947	Manchester City		**1987**	Derby County
1948	Birmingham City		**1988**	Millwall
1949	Fulham		**1989**	Chelsea
1950	Tottenham		**1990**	Leeds United
1951	Preston North End		**1991**	Oldham Athletic
1952	Sheffield Wednesday		**1992**	Ipswich Town

DIVISION ONE WINNERS 1993-2004

1953	Sheffield United			
1954	Leicester City		**1993**	Newcastle United
1955	Birmingham City		**1994**	Crystal Palace
1956	Sheffield Wednesday		**1995**	Middlesbrough
1957	Leicester City		**1996**	Sunderland
1958	West Ham		**1997**	Bolton Wanderers
1959	Sheffield Wednesday		**1998**	Nottingham Forest
1960	Aston Villa		**1999**	Sunderland
1961	Ipswich Town		**2000**	Charlton Athletic
1962	Liverpool		**2001**	Fulham
1963	Stoke City		**2002**	Manchester City
1964	Leeds United		**2003**	Portsmouth
1965	Newcastle United		**2004**	Norwich City

CHAMPIONSHIP WINNERS 2005-12

1966	Manchester City			
1967	Coventry City			
1968	Ipswich Town			
1969	Derby County			
1970	Huddersfield Town		**2005**	Sunderland
1971	Leicester City		**2006**	Reading
1972	Norwich City		**2007**	Sunderland
1973	Burnley		**2008**	West Bromwich Albion
1974	Middlesbrough		**2009**	Wolverhampton Wanderers
1975	Manchester United		**2010**	Newcastle United
1976	Sunderland		**2011**	Queens Park Rangers
1977	Wolverhampton Wanderers		**2012**	Reading
1978	Bolton Wanderers			

BOURNEMOUTH

PLAYERS

MOST APPEARANCES: Steve Fletcher (1992-07, 09-) 712+
MOST GOALS: Ray Eyre (1924-33) 202

Striker Steve Fletcher played all but one game for the Cherries in their 2010 promotion year. He had joined them for his second spell in the January and later took over as club captain. He's a firm favourite with fans and the North Stand was named the Steve Fletcher Stand in April 2010. He plans to retire in 2013. Bournemouth have never risen above the third tier. Their rise to League One in 2010 was remarkable as the previous two seasons they had been deducted 17 points and ten points, the latter costing them relegation from League One.

Founded: 1899
Ground: Dean Court
Capacity: 10,000
Nickname: Cherries

HONOURS

Division Three: 1987
Division Three play-off winners: 2003
Associate Members Cup: 1984

BRENTFORD

PLAYERS

MOST APPEARANCES: Ken Coote (1949-64) 559
MOST GOALS: Jim Towers (1951-61) 163

Midfielder Kevin O'Connor joined Brentford as a 17-year-old in 1999 and has now made more than 450 appearances for the club. In that time he has had 11 managers, suffered three play-off defeats and gone down to League Two in 2007. The Bees won that division in 2009 and agreed a deal with fans' clubs to help safeguard the future of the club.

Founded: 1889
Ground: Griffin Park
Capacity: 12,700
Nickname: Bees

HONOURS

Second Division: 1935
Third Division: 1992
Fourth Division: 1963, 1999, 2009
Third Division (South: 1933

BURY

PLAYERS

MOST APPEARANCES: Norman Bullock (1920-35) 539
MOST GOALS: Craig Madden (1978-86) 153

Entrants into the League in 1894, Bury were promoted at the first attempt and are now one of the longest-serving members of the Football League. Since being relegated from the First Division in 1928 they have never appeared in the top-flight again. Incredibly, Bury were the first club to score 1,000 goals in each of the top four tiers of English football.

Founded: 1885
Ground: Gigg Lane
Capacity: 11,800
Nickname: Shakers

HONOURS

Second Division: 1895
Third Division: 1961
Second Division: 1997
FA Cup: 1900, 1903

CARLISLE UNITED

PLAYERS

MOST LEAGUE APPEARANCES: Allan Ross (1963-79) 466
MOST GOALS: Jimmy McConnell (1928-32) 133

Carlisle joined the Football League in 1928 and have played in every division, even reaching the heights of the old Division One (now Premier League) in 1974-75. They were relegated to the Conference in 2004 but have been in League One since 2006, only missing promotion to the Championship in 2008, when they lost the play-off semi-finals to Leeds.

Founded: 1904
Ground: Brunton Park
Capacity: 18,200
Nickname: Cumbrians, Blues

HONOURS

League Two: 2006
Division Three: 1965, 1995
Football League Trophy: 1997, 2011
Conference play-off winners: 2005

COLCHESTER UNITED

PLAYERS

MOST APPEARANCES: Micky Cook (1969-84) 700
MOST GOALS: Tony Adcock (1981-87, 95-98) 149

Colchester entered the old Third Division South in 1950 and played in Division Three or Four until relegation to the Conference in 1991. They won that division at the second time of asking and climbed to Division Two for 1998-99. They spent two seasons in the Championship from 2006-08 before relegation to League One.

Founded: 1937
Ground: Community Stadium
Capacity: 10,000
Nickname: U's

HONOURS

Third Division play-off winners: 1998
Conference: 1992
FA Trophy: 1972

COVENTRY CITY

PLAYERS

MOST APPEARANCES: Steve Ogrizovic (1984-00) 601
MOST GOALS: Clarrie Burton (1931-37) 182

Founding members of the Premier League, Coventry City were relegated in 2001 to the Championship. They had been in Division One – the forerunner of the Premier League – since 1967, having risen steadily through the leagues. They moved from Highfield Road, their home for 106 years, to the purpose-built Ricoh Arena in 2005. They were relegated to League One in 2012.

Founded: 1883
Ground: Ricoh Arena
Capacity: 32,600
Nickname: Sky Blues

HONOURS

Division Two: 1967
Division Three: 1964
FA Cup: 1987

CRAWLEY TOWN

PLAYERS

MOST APPEARANCES: John Maggs (1963-73, 75-79) 652
MOST GOALS: Phil Basey (1968-7) 107

Big money backing has seen the Sussex side rise in just two seasons from the Conference as champions and then into League One from the third automatic promotion spot in League Two. Yet in 1962 they were just a semi-pro team and as recently as 2004 were playing in the Premier Division of the Southern League.

Founded: 1896
Ground: Broadfield Stadium
Capacity: 5,900
Nickname: Reds, Red Devils

HONOURS

Conference: 2012
Southern League: 2004

CREWE ALEXANDRA

PLAYERS

MOST APPEARANCES: Tommy Lowry (1966-78) 482
MOST GOALS: Herbert Swindells (1928-37) 137

Founding members of the Football League in 1892, Alex departed four years later and didn't return until 1921. Spent 1997-02 in Division One, their highest-ever ranking. Famed for producing quality players from their academy, the side returned to League One after a three-year break following a 2-0 victory over Cheltenham Town in the 2012 League Two play-off final.

Founded: 1877
Ground: Gresty Road
Capacity: 10,150
Nickname: Alex, Railwaymen

HONOURS

League Two play-off winners: 2012
Division Two play-off winners: 1997
Welsh Cup: 1936, 1937

DONCASTER ROVERS

PLAYERS

MOST APPEARANCES: Fred Emery (1925-36) 439
MOST GOALS: Tom Keetley (1923-29) 186

Doncaster's rise up the football ladder over the past decade is remarkable. Having spent most of their existence in the third, fourth and fifth tiers of English football, Donny ended five years in the Conference by winning the play-off final in 2003. They were promoted after their first year back as a League side, spent four seasons in League One and then won a spot in the Championship through the play-offs in 2008. Relegated to League One in 2012.

Founded: 1879
Ground: Keepmoat Stadium
Capacity: 15,200
Nickname: Rovers, Vikings

HONOURS
Division Four: 1966, 1969
Conference play-off winners: 2003
Division Three: 2004
League One play-off winners: 2008
Football League Trophy: 2007

HARTLEPOOL UNITED

PLAYERS

MOST APPEARANCES: Ritchie Humphreys (2001-) 500+
MOST GOALS: Joshie Fletcher (1908-13) 111

The club made infamous by a monkey! During the First World War a monkey was washed up on the local beach and then hanged from the club's goalposts as a spy. At one time the suit of their mascot, H'Angus Monkey, was worn by the local mayor. More famously, this is the club where the legendary Brian Clough began his managerial career. They have always played in the two bottom tiers.

Founded: 1908
Ground: Victoria Park
Capacity: 7,800
Nickname: Pools

HONOURS
Third Division runners-up: 2003
League Two runners-up: 2007

LEYTON ORIENT

PLAYERS

MOST APPEARANCES: Peter Allen (1965-78) 490
MOST GOALS: Tommy Johnston (1956-58, 59-61) 123

Orient spent just one season in England's top-flight in 1962-63. Sold for just £5 in 1995, it is now run by snooker and boxing promoter Barry Hearn. They arrived in League One in 2006, their first time out of the bottom flight in 11 years.

Founded: 1881
Ground: Matchroom Stadium
Capacity: 9,270
Nickname: Orient, O's

HONOURS
Division Three: 1970
Division Three South: 1956

MK DONS

PLAYERS

MOST APPEARANCES: Dean Lewington 400+ (2004-)
MOST GOALS: Izale McLeod (2004-07) 54

MK Dons was formed when the former Wimbledon FC went into administration following relegation to League One in 2004. The original club had moved to Milton Keynes Hockey Stadium from its South West London home in 2003 and changed its name when it was taken over by Pete Winkelman in 2004. The Dons spent two seasons in League Two before promotion back to One in 2008.

Founded: 2004
Ground: Stadium MK
Capacity: 22,000
Nickname: Dons

HONOURS
League Two: 2008
Football League Trophy: 200

NOTTS COUNTY

PLAYERS

MOST APPEARANCES: Albert Iremonger (1904-26) 601
MOST GOALS: Les Bradd (1967-78) 137

The oldest professional football club in the world, County even inspired the legendary Italian side Juventus to base its strip on the Magpies' famous black and white shirts. The club's financial problems and the arrival of former England manager Sven Goran Eriksson as Director of Football in 2009 raised County's status further. The boss lasted just over six months before quitting – the team still being promoted as League Two champions under Steve Cotterill.

Founded: 1862
Ground: Meadow Lane
Capacity: 20,200
Nickname: Magpies

HONOURS

Division Two: 1897, 1914, 1923 **Fourth Division:** 1971 **Third Division:** 1998 **League Two:** 2010 **Second Division play-offs:** 1991 **Third Division play-offs:** 1990 **FA Cup:** 1894

OLDHAM ATHLETIC

PLAYERS

MOST LEAGUE APPEARANCES: Ian Wood (1966-80) 525
MOST LEAGUE GOALS: Roger Palmer (1980-92) 141

First Division runners-up in 1914-15, Oldham have spent most of their time in the lower leagues since 1923. In 1991 they gained promotion to the top-flight for the first time in 68 years but were relegated after three seasons, two in the Premier League of which they were a founder member. Three-times losing FA Cup semi-finalists they were also beaten in the 1990 final of the Football League Cup.

Founded: 1895
Ground: Boundary Park
Capacity: 10,600
Nickname: Latics

HONOURS

Second Division: 1991
Third Division: 1974

PORTSMOUTH

PLAYERS

MOST APPEARANCES: Jimmy Dickinson (1946-65) 834
MOST GOALS: Peter Harris (1946-60) 211

Just a few years after almost folding due to financial problems, Portsmouth were promoted to the Premier League in 2003 under the guidance of Harry Redknapp. The manager left for a brief spell in charge of rivals Southampton before returning to take them to FA Cup glory. But he left in 2008 and at the end of 2009-10 Pompey dropped into the Championship with crippling debts. A points deduction for more financial problems in 2011-12 saw them relegated to League One.

Founded: 1898
Ground: Fratton Park
Capacity: 20,200
Nickname: Pompey, Blues

HONOURS

League Champions: 1949, 1950
First Division: 2003
Third Division: 1924, 1962, 1983
FA Cup: 1939, 2008
Charity Shield: 1949

PRESTON NORTH END

PLAYERS

MOST APPEARANCES: Alan Kelly (1958-73) 447
MOST GOALS: Tom Finney (1946-60) 210

The first-ever League Champions and a founder member of the Football League, North End went the whole of their first season unbeaten. They were also the first side to do the Double. Relegated to the second tier in 1961, Preston have fallen as low as the fourth tier. Three times in the play-offs, they have yet to play in the Premier League. They were relegated to League One in 2011 after 11 years in the Championship.

Founded: 1881
Ground: Deepdale
Capacity: 23,400
Nickname: North End, Lilywhites

HONOURS

League Champions: 1889, 1890
Second Division: 1904, 1913, 1951
Third Division: 1971, 2000
Fourth Division: 1996
FA Cup: 1889, 1938

PLAYERS

MOST APPEARANCES: Jack Brownsword (1947-65) 791
MOST GOALS: Steve Cammack (1979-81, 82-86) 109

Scunthorpe have never been higher than the second division of League Football but their achievements have been remarkable considering they have a small ground and low attendances. Survival in the Championship after their promotion from League One in 2009 could be regarded as a major success. Having almost lost their league status in 2004, the Iron have since enjoyed three promotions and one relegation.

Founded: 1899
Ground: Glanville Park
Capacity: 9,000
Nickname: Iron

HONOURS

League One: 2007
League One play-off winners: 2009
Division Three play-offs: 1999
Division Three North: 1958

SCUNTHORPE

PLAYERS

MOST APPEARANCES: Joe Shaw (1945-66) 714
MOST GOALS: Harry Johnson (1916-30) 201

Founder members of the Premier League, the Blades were relegated at the end of the competition's second season. They remained in the second tier until they were promoted as Championship runners-up in 2006, having missed out three earlier play-offs, including two finals. United were relegated after just one season and again missed out on promotion when they lost the 2009 play-off final. Relegated to the third tier for the first time in 23 years in 2011 they lost the 2012 League One play-off final to Yorkshire rivals Huddersfield.

Founded: 1889
Ground: Bramall Lane
Capacity: 32,700
Nickname: Blades

HONOURS

League Champions: 1898
Division Two: 1953
Division Four: 1982
FA Cup: 1899, 1902, 1915, 1925

SHEFFIELD UNITED

PLAYERS

MOST LEAGUE APPEARANCES: Mickey Brown (1986-91, 92-94, 96-01) 418
MOST LEAGUE GOALS: Arthur Rowley (1958-65) 152

Football League members since 1950, the Shrews lost their status in 2003. They bounced back at the first attempt, defeating Aldershot Town in a penalty shoot-out in the Conference play-off final. The team lost out 3-1 to Bristol Rovers in the League Two play-off final of 2007. Then they won automatic promotion in 2012 as League Two runners-up.

Founded: 1886
Ground: Greenhous Meadow
Capacity: 9,800
Nickname: Shrews, Blues

HONOURS

Third Division: 1979
Division Three: 1994
Conference play-off winners: 2004
Welsh Cup: 1891, 1938, 1977 1984 1985

SHREWSBURY TOWN

PLAYERS

MOST APPEARANCES: Mark Smith (1992-01, 03-04) 466
MOST GOALS: Mark Gittings (1980-95) 209

Stevenage were promoted through the minor leagues until they reached the Conference in 1994. The club won this division in 1996 but were refused League status as their ground was not up to standard. Boro spent more than £500,000 improving Broadhall Way and after winning the Conference in 2010 were promoted – and dropped the word Borough from their name. Promoted again after beating Torquay 1-0 in the 2011 League Two play-off final.

Founded: 1976
Ground: Broadhall Way
Capacity: 6,700
Nickname: Boro

HONOURS

Conference: 1996, 2010
League Two play-off winners: 2011
FA Trophy: 2007, 2009

STEVENAGE

SWINDON TOWN

PLAYERS

MOST APPEARANCES: John Trollope (1960-80) 886
MOST GOALS: Harry Morris (1926-33) 229

Swindon appeared in the Premier League in 1993-94. They were only the second team to reach the Premiership via the play-offs but their one season stay saw them set an unwanted record with 100 goals against. The following season they were relegated for a second time and went into League Two in 2006. The Robins returned to League One the following season but were relegated in 2011. New boss Paolo Di Canio took them up as League Two champions in 2012.

Founded: 1879
Ground: County Ground
Capacity: 14,700
Nickname: Robins

HONOURS

League Two: 2012 **Fourth Division:** 1986 **Division Two:** 1996 **Third Division play-off winners:** 1987 **Second Division play-off winners:** 1990 **League One play-off winners:** 1993
League Cup: 1969

TRANMERE ROVERS

PLAYERS

MOST APPEARANCES: Ray Mathias (1964-85) 637
MOST GOALS: Ian Muir (1985-95) 180

Rovers entered the newly formed Third Division North in 1921 and won the league in 1938 to earn a place in League Division Two. There followed many years in divisions Three and Four before the club earned a place in Division Two in 1991 via the play-off final. Rovers were relegated from what was the country's second tier in 2001.

Founded: 1884
Ground: Prenton Park
Capacity: 16,500
Nickname: Rovers, Super Whites

HONOURS

Welsh Cup: 1935
Football League Trophy: 1990
Division Three play-off winners: 1991

WALSALL

PLAYERS

MOST APPEARANCES: Jimmy Walker (1993-04, 10-) 531+
MOST GOALS: Alan Buckley (1973-78, 79-84) 202

A founder member of the old Division Two in 1892, Walsall have never appeared in English football's top-flight. They dropped out of the League system in 1895 and eventually became a founder member of the Fourth Division in 1958. Many promotion, relegations and changes of manager later they arrived in League One in 2007.

Founded: 1888
Ground: Banks' Stadium
Capacity: 11,300
Nickname: Saddlers

HONOURS

Division Four: 1960
Division Three play-off winners: 1988
Division Two play-off winners: 2001
League Two: 2007

YEOVIL TOWN

PLAYERS

MOST APPEARANCES: Len Harris (1958-72) 691
MOST GOALS: Johnny Hayward (1906-28) 548

Famous for their FA Cup giant-killing acts whilst a non-league side, Yeovil also gained recognition for their equally famed sloping pitch! Their rapid rise up the league system after winning the Conference could have been even more remarkable as they reached the League One play-off final in 2007 only to be beaten 2-0 by Blackpool.

Founded: 1895
Ground: Huish Park
Capacity: 9,600
Nickname: Glovers

HONOURS

Conference: 2003
League Two: 2005
FA Trophy: 2002

ENGLAND'S THIRD TIER

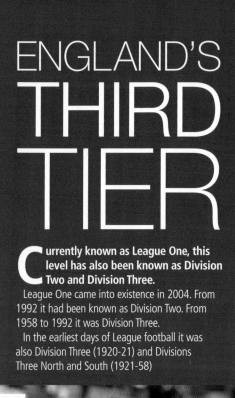

Currently known as League One, this level has also been known as Division Two and Division Three.

League One came into existence in 2004. From 1992 it had been known as Division Two. From 1958 to 1992 it was Division Three.

In the earliest days of League football it was also Division Three (1920-21) and Divisions Three North and South (1921-58)

2012

ALL THE WINNERS...

THIRD DIVISION
1921	Crystal Palace

THIRD DIVISION NORTH/SOUTH
1922	Stockport County	Southampton
1923	Nelson	Bristol City
1924	Wolverhampton	Portsmouth
1925	Darlington	Swansea City
1926	Grimsby Town	Reading
1927	Stoke City	Bristol City
1928	Bradford Park Avenue	Millwall
1929	Bradford City	Charlton Athletic
1930	Port Vale	Plymouth Argyle
1931	Chesterfield	Notts County
1932	Lincoln City	Fulham
1933	Hull City	Brentford
1934	Barnsley	Norwich City
1935	Doncaster Rovers	Charlton Athletic
1936	Chesterfield	Coventry City
1937	Stockport County	Luton Town
1938	Tranmere Rovers	Millwall
1939	Barnsley	Newport County
1939-46	World War II	
1947	Doncaster Rovers	Cardiff City
1948	Lincoln City	Queens Park Rangers
1949	Hull City	Swansea City
1950	Doncaster Rovers	Notts County

1991

1951	Rotherham United	Nottingham Forest	**1987**	Bournemouth
1952	Lincoln City	Plymouth Argyle	**1988**	Sunderland
1953	Oldham Athletic	Bristol Rovers	**1989**	Wolverhampton Wanderers
1954	Port Vale	Ipswich Town	**1990**	Bristol Rovers
1955	Barnsley	Bristol City	**1991**	Cambridge United
1956	Grimsby Town	Leyton Orient	**1992**	Brentford
1957	Derby County	Ipswich Town		
1958	Scunthorpe United	Brighton and Hove Albion		

THIRD DIVISION

1959 Plymouth Argyle
1960 Southampton
1961 Bury
1962 Portsmouth
1963 Northampton Town
1964 Coventry City
1965 Carlisle United
1966 Hull City
1967 Queens Park Rangers
1968 Oxford United
1969 Watford
1970 Leyton Orient
1971 Preston North End
1972 Aston Villa
1973 Bolton Wanderers
1974 Oldham Athletic
1975 Blackburn Rovers
1976 Hereford United
1977 Mansfield Town
1978 Wrexham
1979 Shrewsbury Town
1980 Grimsby Town
1981 Rotherham United
1982 Burnley
1983 Portsmouth
1984 Oxford United
1985 Bradford City
1986 Reading

1993

SECOND DIVISION

1993 Stoke City
1994 Reading
1995 Birmingham City
1996 Swindon Town
1997 Bury
1998 Watford
1999 Fulham
2000 Preston North End
2001 Millwall
2002 Brighton and Hove Albion
2003 Wigan Athletic
2004 Plymouth Argyle

LEAGUE ONE

2005 Luton Town
2006 Southend United
2007 Scunthorpe United
2008 Swansea City
2009 Leicester City
2010 Norwich City
2011 Brighton and Hove Albion
2012 Charlton Athletic

ACCRINGTON STANLEY

PLAYERS

MOST LEAGUE APPEARANCES:
Jim Armstrong (1927-34) 260
MOST LEAGUE GOALS: George Stewart (1954-58) 136

Promoted as Conference champions in 2006, Stanley re-entered the League after a 44-year absence. The original club, formed in 1891, was in League football from 1921 to 1961 before it went bust and dropped into non-league football. Stanley then had to start in local leagues and win its way back up the football pyramid, thanks to the backing of local businessman Eric Whalley.

Founded: 1968
Ground: Crown Ground
Capacity: 5,000
Nickname: Accies, Stanley, Reds

HONOURS
Conference: 2006
Northern Premier League: 2003

AFC WIMBLEDON

PLAYERS

MOST APPEARANCES: Sam Hatton (2007-12) 241
MOST GOALS: Kevin Cooper (2002-04) 107

AFC was formed when the original Wimbledon moved to Milton Keynes. The club started in the Combined Counties Premier League and after five promotions in nine seasons reached the Football League. Between February 2003 and December 2004 the Dons went a record 78 consecutive league matches without defeat.

Founded: 2002
Ground: Kingsmeadow
Capacity: 4,700
Nickname: Dons, Phoenix

HONOURS
Conference play-off winners: 2011
Conference South: 2009
Isthmian League 1: 2005
Combined Counties Prem: 2004

ALDERSHOT TOWN

PLAYERS

MOST APPEARANCES: Jason Chewins (1994-04) 489
MOST GOALS: Mark Butler (1992-98) 155

Fourth Division (League Two) Aldershot FC went bust in 1992 having been a League club since 1932, and a founder member of the lowest tier. The Shots were the first League side to fold since Accrington in 1962. Aldershot Town rose from the remains of FC and worked its way back to League football in 2008 from five divisions lower.

Founded: 1992
Ground: Recreation Ground
Capacity: 7,100
Nickname: Shots

HONOURS
Conference: 2008
Conference League Cup: 2008

BARNET

PLAYERS

MOST LEAGUE APPEARANCES:
Les Eason (1965-74, 77-78) 648
MOST LEAGUE GOALS: Arthur Morris (1927-36) 403

Barnet's first venture into League football came when they won promotion from the Conference to Division Four in 1991. They did get as high as the new Division Two before losing their League status ten years later in 2001. After a four-year spell in the Conference, Barnet returned to League Two in 2005. Season 2011-12 saw them survive on the final day for the third successive year.

Founded: 1888
Ground: Underhill
Capacity: 5,200
Nickname: Bees

HONOURS
Conference: 1991, 2005
Amateur Cup: 1946

BRADFORD CITY

PLAYERS

MOST APPEARANCES: Ces Podd (1970-84) 565
MOST GOALS: Bobby Campbell (1979-83, 83-86) 143

Bradford City went straight into League Division Two after the club was founded and within five years was in Division One. Paul Jewell guided the Bantams to the Premier League in 1999, the club's first appearance in the top-flight in 77 years. The side stayed there for two seasons but after financial problems suffered three relegations in seven seasons and started 2007-08 in League Two.

Founded: 1903
Ground: Valley Parade
Capacity: 25,100
Nickname: Bantams

HONOURS

Division Two: 1908
Division Three: 1985
Division Two play-off winners: 1996
FA Cup: 1911

BRISTOL ROVERS

PLAYERS

MOST LEAGUE APPEARANCES: Stuart Taylor (1965-80) 546
MOST GOALS: Geoff Bradford (1949-64) 242

Rovers' best-ever finish was sixth spot (twice) in Division Two – now known as The Championship – in 1956 and 1959. Having played at the fourth level of English League football for the first time in 2001 Rovers escaped the drop into the Conference despite finishing second bottom as just one team was relegated. The Pirates arrived back in League One in 2007 only to be relegated in 2011.

Founded: 1883
Ground: Memorial Stadium
Capacity: 12,000
Nickname: Pirates, The Gas

HONOURS

Division Three: 1990
League Two play-off winners: 2007

BURTON ALBION

PLAYERS

MOST APPEARANCES: Darren Stride (1993-10) 646
MOST GOALS: Richie Barker (1960-62, 63-67) 159

Burton Albion arrived in the Football League in 2009-10 – the club having risen from the ashes of former league clubs Burton Swifts, Burton United and Burton Wanderers. Albion began in 1950. Former Derby defender Roy McFarland managed them into the league but was then not handed a contract.

Founded: 1950
Ground: Pirelli Stadium
Capacity: 6,900
Nickname: Brewers

HONOURS

Conference: 2009
Northern Premier League: 2002

CHELTENHAM TOWN

PLAYERS

MOST APPEARANCES: Roger Thorndale (1958-76) 702
MOST GOALS: Dave Lewis (1967-83) 290*

League members since they won the Conference in 1999 under Steve Cotterill, Cheltenham have since enjoyed two promotions to Division Two (now League One). They were relegated back to League Two in 2009. Lost to Crewe in the 2012 play-off final.
*As an amateur, Reg Smith bagged 300+ goals for the Robins.

Founded: 1887
Ground: Abbey Business Stadium
Capacity: 7,000
Nickname: Robins

HONOURS

Conference: 1999
FA Trophy: 1998
Division Three play-off winners: 2002, 2006

CHESTERFIELD

PLAYERS

MOST APPEARANCES: Dave Blakey (1948-67) 617
MOST LEAGUE GOALS:
Ernie Moss (1968-75, 79-81, 84-86) 162

The Football League's fourth-oldest club, having joined in 1899, the Robins reached as high as fourth in the old Division Two (Championship) in 1947. Otherwise, they have spent most of their life in the two lowest tiers of English football. The Spireites moved to their new ground in summer 2010 and were relegated to League Two in 2012.

Founded: 1867
Ground: B2Net Stadium
Capacity: 10,400
Nickname: Spireites

HONOURS

League Two: 2011
Third Division play-off winners: 1995
Fourth Division: 1970, 1985
Third Division North: 1931, 1936
Football League Trophy: 2012

DAGENHAM & REDBRIDGE

PLAYERS

MOST APPEARANCES: Tony Roberts (2000-11) 507
MOST GOALS: Danny Shipp (1997-04) 102

The Daggers were formed by local sides Leytonstone, Ilford and Walthamstow Avenue all merging to form Redbridge Forest. They then joined forces with Dagenham to create the club in 1992. John Still was at the helm and despite a period away returned to take the side back into the League in 2007 and then further promotion in 2010. The club was relegated from League One in 2011.

Founded: 1992
Ground: Victoria Road
Capacity: 6,000
Nickname: Daggers

HONOURS

Conference: 2007
League Two play-off winners: 2010

EXETER CITY

PLAYERS

MOST APPEARANCES: Arnold Mitchell (1948-65) 495
MOST GOALS: Tony Kellow (1976-78, 80-84, 85-88) 129

Exeter City, owned by a supporters' trust, spent five seasons in the Conference before winning the play-off final in 2008. The Grecians earned automatic promotion to League One in their first season but were relegated in 2012. Before dropping into non-league in 2003, Exeter had been in the lower divisions of the Football League since 1920.

Founded: 1904
Ground: St. James' Park
Capacity: 8,500
Nickname: Grecians

HONOURS

Fourth Division: 1990
Conference play-off winners: 2008

FLEETWOOD TOWN

PLAYERS

MOST APPEARANCES: Percy Ronson (1949-64) 416
MOST GOALS: Jamie Vardy (2011-12) 34

Although reformed in 1997, the club was first created in 1908. The Cod Army won promotion to the Football League for the first time ever with two Conference games to spare and the club's 2011-12 season included a 29-game unbeaten run in the fifth tier of English football. *Vardy scored his goals in 36 games over 247 days with Town before a move to Leicester City. There are no official club records for Fleetwood's all-time leading scorer.

Founded: 1997
Ground: Highbury
Capacity: 5,000
Nickname: Trawlermen, Cod Army

HONOURS

Conference: 2012

GILLINGHAM

PLAYERS

MOST APPEARANCES: Ron Hillyard (1974-90) 657
MOST GOALS: Brian Yeo (1963-75) 136

The Gills appeared in the Football League in 1920, were voted out in 1938, then returned in 1950 when the divisions were expanded. The Gills survived a financial crisis in 1995 and reached Division One (now Championship) in 2000 and stayed to 2005. They slipped into League One in 2004, were relegated again in 2008, promoted back to League One in 2009 and dropped back into League Two in 2010.

Founded: 1893
Ground: Priestfield
Capacity: 11,500
Nickname: Gills

HONOURS

Division Two play-off winners: 2000
League Two play-off winners: 2009
Fourth Division: 1964

MORECAMBE

PLAYERS

MOST APPEARANCES: Steve Done (1968-78) 530
MOST GOALS: Keith Borrowdale (1958-68, 78-79) 289

Morecambe beat Exeter City at Wembley in the 2007 Conference play-off final to win promotion to the Football League for the first time ever. There were 40,000 fans at the game, 10,000 of them backing the Seasiders. The Shrimps moved to their new ground from Christie Park in 2010.

Founded: 1920
Ground: Globe Arena
Capacity: 6,400
Nickname: Shrimps

HONOURS

Conference play-off winners: 2007
FA Trophy: 1974

NORTHAMPTON TOWN

PLAYERS

MOST APPEARANCES: Tommy Fowler (1946-61) 552
MOST GOALS: Jack English (1947-59) 143

It took Northampton just five seasons – a record – to be promoted from the old Fourth Division to the top-flight, but the Cobblers spent just one season in the old Division One, 1965-66. Infamously, Town lost an FA Cup tie to Manchester United in 1970 in which George Best scored six goals. The club nearly lost its league status in 1994 when it finished bottom – reprieved only because the ground of Conference winners Kidderminster didn't shape up.

Founded: 1897
Ground: Sixfields
Capacity: 7,600
Nickname: Cobblers

HONOURS

Fourth Division: 1987
Third Division: 1963
Fourth Division play-off winners: 1997

OXFORD UNITED

PLAYERS

MOST LEAGUE APPEARANCES: John Shuker (1962-77) 478
MOST GOALS: Graham Atkinson (1962-74) 107

Oxford United first entered the Football League in 1962 and reached the top-flight – the old First Division – in 1986. The club stayed there two years but then fell down the leagues and into the Conference in 2006. United beat York City in the play-off final to regain League status in 2010. Despite the club's League Cup win it did not play in Europe because of a ban on English teams at the time.

Founded: 1893
Ground: Kassam Stadium
Capacity: 12,500
Nickname: Us, Yellows

HONOURS

Second Division: 1985
Third Division: 1968, 1984
Conference play-off winners: 2010
League Cup: 1986

PLYMOUTH ARGYLE

PLAYERS

MOST APPEARANCES: Kevin Hodges (1978-92) 620
MOST GOALS: Sammy Black (1924-38) 184

The furthest south League club in England, Plymouth is the biggest city in the country never to appear in the top-flight. Having joined the Football League in 1920 the Pilgrims spent 41 of those years in the second-flight, before being relegated to League One at the end of season 2009-10 and then dropped straight into League Two.

Founded: 1886
Ground: Home Park
Capacity: 16,300
Nickname: Pilgrims, Argyle

HONOURS

Division Two: 2004
Third Division: 1959, 2002
Third Division play-off winners: 1996

PORT VALE

PLAYERS

MOST APPEARANCES: Roy Sproson (1949-72) 842
MOST GOALS: Wilf Kirkham (1923-29, 32-33) 164

Vale have never finished higher than eighth in the second tier of English football, reaching that spot in the First Division of 1997. Rock star Robbie Williams is a fan and shareholder and some of his cash helped them through financial difficulties in the early 2000s. The club slumped to League Two in 2009 for the first time in more than 20 years.

Founded: 1876
Ground: Vale Park
Capacity: 19,000
Nickname: Vale, Valliants

HONOURS

Third Division play-off winners: 1989
Fourth Division: 1959
Football League Trophy: 1993, 2001

ROCHDALE

PLAYERS

MOST APPEARANCES: Gary Jones (1998-01, 2004-12) 531
MOST LEAGUE GOALS: Reg Jenkins 129 (1964-73)

Football League members since 1921, Rochdale have only ever been out of the bottom tier on two occasions, winning promotions in 1969 and 2010. They are the only bottom tier club to have appeared in the League Cup Final, beaten 4-0 by Norwich City in 1962. Dale were relegated back to League Two in 2012.

Founded: 1907
Ground: Spotland
Capacity: 10,200
Nickname: Dale

HONOURS

League Two: 2010 (third)
Division Four: 1969 (third)

ROTHERHAM UNITED

PLAYERS

MOST APPEARANCES: Danny Williams (1945-66) 621
MOST LEAGUE GOALS: Gladstone Guest (1946-56) 130

Housed in Sheffield's Don Valley Stadium until they awaited their new ground to replace Millmoor, Rotherham missed out on reaching the top-flight on goal difference in 1955. They have played in the old Second Division and more recently the Championship. Despite financial restraints, the club reached the League Two play-off final in 2010 losing out 3-2 to Dagenham and Redbridge.

Founded: 1888
Ground: New York Stadium
Capacity: 12,000
Nickname: Millers

HONOURS

Third Division: 1981
Fourth Division: 1989
Football League Trophy: 199

SOUTHEND UNITED

PLAYERS

MOST APPEARANCES: Alan Moody (1972-84) 506
MOST GOALS: Roy Hollis (1954-60) 135

The Shrimpers joined the Football League in 1920 and spent most of their days in the bottom two flights, surviving a battle against financial extinction in the 1980s. In 1991 they arrived in the old Second Division for the first time ever and spent six seasons there. There were more relegations before promotion to the Championship in 2006 for one year, followed by more drops down the divisions. They arrived in League Two in 2010. A new ground is planned.

Founded: 1906
Ground: Roots Hall
Capacity: 12,300
Nickname: Shrimpers, Blues

HONOURS

League One: 2006
League Two play-off winners: 2005
Fourth Division: 1981

TORQUAY UNITED

PLAYERS

MOST APPEARANCES: Kevin Hill (1997-08) 474
MOST GOALS: Sammy Collins (1948-58) 219

Torquay spent 82 years in the League before relegation and then two seasons in the Conference between 2007-09. They began in Division Three (South) in 1927 and have spent the rest of their League career in English football's bottom two tiers. Ground development reduced capacity for season 2011-12.

Founded: 1899
Ground: Plainmoor
Capacity: 6,100
Nickname: Gulls

HONOURS

Fourth Division play-off winners: 1991
Conference play-off winners: 2009

WYCOMBE WANDERERS

PLAYERS

MOST APPEARANCES: Tony Horseman (1961-78) 749
MOST GOALS: Tony Horseman (1961-78) 416

After a proud tradition in amateur and non-league football, Wycombe finally won the Conference in 1992-93 and were promoted to Division Three. They won promotion in their first season, beating Preston in the play-off final. In 2001 they reached the semi-finals of the FA Cup. They have since spent time in both of the two bottom tiers, relegated to League Two in 2012.

Founded: 1887
Ground: Adams Park
Capacity: 10,200
Nickname: Chairboys, Blues

HONOURS

Division Three play-off winners: 1994
Conference: 1993
FA Trophy: 1991, 1993
Amateur Cup: 1931

YORK CITY

PLAYERS

MOST APPEARANCES: Barry Jackson (1956-70) 539
MOST GOALS: Norman Wilkinson (1954-66) 143

After eight seasons in the Conference, City returned to League Two at the end of 2011-12 through the play-off final. They also bagged the FA Trophy. York have been as high as the second tier of English football but have spend most of their League life in the bottom two divisions. They are famed for a 3-0 League Cup win at Old Trafford in 1995-96 and a 1985 FA Cup victory over Arsenal.

Founded: 1922
Ground: Bootham Crescent
Capacity: 7,800
Nickname: Minstermen

HONOURS

Conference play-off winners: 2012
Fourth Division: 1984
League Two play-off winners: 1993
FA Trophy: 2012

1975

1988

1999

ENGLAND'S FOURTH TIER

Currently known as League Two, this level has also been known as Division Three and Division Four.

League Two came into existence in 2004. From 1992 it had been known as Division Three. From 1958 to 1992 it was Division Four. It was originally formed from the merging of the Third Divsions North and South

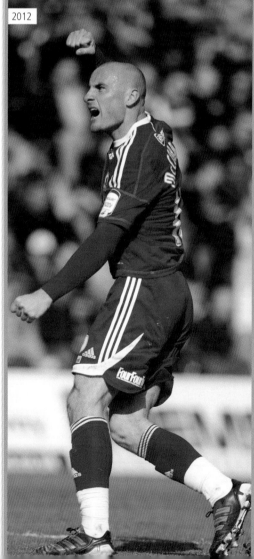

2012

ALL THE WINNERS...

FOURTH DIVISION

1959 Port Vale
1960 Walsall
1961 Peterborough United
1962 Millwall
1963 Brentford
1964 Gillingham
1965 Brighton and Hove Albion
1966 Doncaster Rovers
1967 Stockport County
1968 Luton Town
1969 Doncaster Rovers
1970 Chesterfield
1971 Notts County
1972 Grimsby Town
1973 Southport
1974 Peterborough United
1975 Mansfield Town
1976 Lincoln City
1977 Cambridge United
1978 Watford
1979 Reading
1980 Huddersfield Town
1981 Southend United
1982 Sheffield United
1983 Wimbledon
1984 York City
1985 Chesterfield
1986 Swindon Town

2011

1987 Northampton Town
1988 Wolverhampton Wanderers
1989 Rotherham United
1990 Exeter City
1991 Darlington
1992 Burnley

2012

THIRD DIVISION

1993 Cardiff City
1994 Shrewsbury Town
1995 Carlisle United
1996 Preston North End
1997 Wigan Athletic
1998 Notts County
1999 Brentford
2000 Swansea City
2001 Brighton and Hove Albion
2002 Plymouth Argle
2003 Rushden and Diamonds
2004 Doncaster Rovers

LEAGUE TWO

2005 Yeovil Town
2006 Carlisle United
2007 Walsall
2008 MK Dons
2009 Brentford
2010 Notts County
2011 Chesterfield
2012 Swindon Town

GLASGOW CELTIC

Jimmy McGrory

Founded: 1887   Ground: Celtic Park
Capacity: 60,800   Nickname: Bhoys, Hoops

HONOURS

League Champions (43): 1893, 1894, 1896, 1898, 1905, 1906, 1907, 1908, 1909, 1910, 1914, 1915, 1916, 1917, 1919, 1922, 1926, 1936, 1938, 1954, 1966. 1967, 1968, 1969, 1970, 1971, 1972, 1973, 1974, 1977, 1979, 1981, 1982, 1986, 1988, 1998, 2001, 2002, 2004, 2006, 2007, 2008, 2012
Scottish FA Cup (35): 1892, 1899, 1900, 1904, 1907, 1908, 1911, 1912, 1914, 1923, 1925, 1927, 1931, 1933, 1937, 1951, 1954, 1965, 1967, 1969, 1971, 1972, 1974, 1975, 1977, 1980, 1985, 1988, 1989, 1995, 2001, 2004, 2005, 2007, 2011
Scottish League Cup (14): 1957, 1958, 1966, 1967, 1968, 1969, 1970, 1975, 1983, 1998, 2000, 2001, 2006, 2009
European Cup: 1967

PLAYERS

MOST APPEARANCES:
Billy McNeil (1957-75) 790

MOST GOALS:
Jimmy McGrory (1922-38) 522

FAN FAVOURITE:
Scott Brown (2007-)
The club's captain and Scotland midfielder was a £4.4m buy from Hibs – a record fee between two Scottish clubs. The Bhoys reportedly turned down the chance to double that amount when they rejected a Portsmouth bid to take the player south. Primarily a defensive midfielder, Brown has become an influential player who also weighs in with a few goals.

The arrival of Neil Lennon as boss in 2010 meant he became only the 18th manager of Celtic in their history. In post-War years only one manager really stands out in Bhoys history, Jock Stein who won ten titles for them between 1965 and 1978. He also added eight FA Cups, six League Cups and their one and only European Cup. Billy McNeil, Martin O'Neill and Gordon Strachan have all weighed in with three titles each as Celtic battle to try and catch up with Glasgow rivals Rangers.

Scott Brown

PLAYERS

MOST APPEARANCES:
John Greig (1961-78) 755

MOST GOALS:
Ally McCoist (1983-98) 355

FAN FAVOURITE: David Weir (2007-12)
The veteran defender reached his 41st birthday in May 2011 and was still playing for both club and country. Having started his career in Scotland with Falkirk and Hearts he moved to Everton where he made a major impression. Capped 69 times by Scotland, Weir returned across the border to team up with Walter Smith – a boss who had earlier tempted him out of international retirement. Left Rangers in January 2012 to coach at Everton.

Rangers have 54 league titles to their credit – a world record. They have also won the Scottish Cup more times than any other side and in 1961 became the first British club to reach the final of a UEFA competition when they played in the Cup Winners' Cup. Their most successful manager was Bill Struth with 18 titles, ten FA Cups and two League Cups between 1920 and 1954. In recent years Walter Smith, who has had two spells with the Gers, has won 10 titles, six FA Cups and five League Cups, making him their second most successful boss. Financial problems hit Rangers in 2012 and led to the formation of a new club.

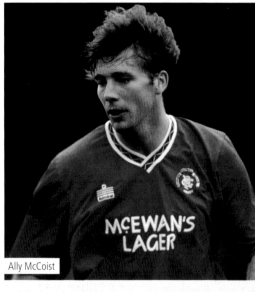

Ally McCoist

Founded: 1873   **Ground:** Ibrox
Capacity: 51,082   **Nickname:** Gers, Blues,

HONOURS

League Champions (54): 1891, 1899, 1900, 1901, 1902, 1911, 1912, 1913, 1918, 1920, 1921, 1923, 1924, 1925, 1927, 1928, 1929, 1930, 1931, 1933, 1934, 1935, 1937, 1939, 1947, 1949, 1950, 1953, 1956, 1957, 1959, 1961, 1963, 1964, 1975, 1976, 1978, 1987, 1989, 1990. 1991, 1992, 1993, 1994, 1995, 1996, 1997, 1999, 2000, 2003, 2005, 2009, 2010, 2011
Scottish FA Cup: (33): 1894, 1897, 1898, 1903, 1928, 1930, 1932, 1934, 1935, 1936, 1948, 1949, 1950, 1953, 1960, 1962, 1963, 1964, 1966, 1973, 1976, 1978, 1979, 1981, 1992, 1993, 1996, 1999, 2000, 2002, 2003, 2008, 2009
Scottish League Cup (27): 1947, 1949, 1961, 1962, 1964, 1965, 1971, 1976, 1978, 1979, 1982, 1984, 1985, 1987, 1988, 1989, 1991, 1993, 1994, 1997, 1999, 2002, 2003, 2005, 2008, 2010, 2011
Cup Winners' Cup: 1972

David Weir

GLASGOW RANGERS

ABERDEEN

PLAYERS

MOST APPEARANCES: Willie Miller (1972-90) 797
MOST GOALS: Joe Harper (1969-81) 199

There's no doubt about Aberdeen's most successful manager – current Manchester United boss Sir Alex Ferguson. Fergie was in charge of the Dons from 1978 to 1986 and in that time they won three league titles, four FA Cups and a League Cup plus the European Cup Winners' Cup and European Super Cup. The Dons only just retained their Premier League status in 2000 when Falkirk were refused entry because their stadium was not up to standard.

Founded: 1903
Ground: Pittodrie
Capacity: 22,200
Nickname: Dons, Dandies, Reds

HONOURS

League Champions: 1955, 1980, 1984, 1985 **Scottish FA Cup:** 1947, 1970, 1982, 1983, 1984, 1986, 1990 **Scottish League Cup:** 1956, 1977, 1986, 1990, 1996 **European Cup Winners Cup:** 1983 **European Super Cup:** 1983

DUNDEE UNITED

PLAYERS

MOST APPEARANCES: David Narey (1973-94) 865
MOST GOALS: Peter McKay (1947-54) 201

Founder members of the Scottish Premier League in 1998, Dundee United played 14 consecutive seasons in Europe from 1976, during that time reaching the final of the UEFA Cup and semi-finals of the European Cup. They have provided some noted Scotland players over the years, including Richard Hough, Paul Sturrock and Duncan Ferguson.

Founded: 1909
Ground: Tannadice
Capacity: 14,200
Nickname: Terrors, Tangerines

HONOURS

League Champions: 1983 **Division Two:** 1925, 1929 **Scottish FA Cup:** 1994, 2010 **Scottish League Cup:** 1980, 1981

HEART OF MIDLOTHIAN

PLAYERS

MOST APPEARANCES: Gary Mackay (1980-97) 640
MOST GOALS: John Robertson (1981-88, 88-98) 214

Edinburgh's oldest club and big rivals with Hibernian. Lithuanian Vladimir Romanov took over the club in 2005 and with his arrival came a number of managerial changes and many players from his home country. The owner was also accused of picking the team! The sight of fans twirling their scarves is believed to have started life at Tynecastle.

Founded: 1874
Ground: Tynecastle
Capacity: 17,400
Nickname: Hearts, Jam Tarts, Jambos

HONOURS

League Champions: 1895, 1897, 1958, 1960 **Scottish FA Cup:** 1891, 1896, 1901, 1906, 1956, 1998, 2006, 2012 **Scottish League Cup:** 1955, 1959, 1960, 1963

HIBERNIAN

PLAYERS

MOST LEAGUE APPEARANCES: Arthur Duncan (1969-84) 446
MOST GOALS: Lawrie Reilly (1946-58) 232

Although Edinburgh rivals Hearts have the edge in winning the city derby, the biggest victory in that clash was Hibs 7-0 win in 1973. One of the top four in terms of crowd attendances, Hibs have been members of the Scottish Premier League in all but its very first season, being promoted to the competition in 1999.

Founded: 1875
Ground: Easter Road
Capacity: 20,400
Nickname: Hibs, Hibbees

HONOURS

League Champions: 1903, 1948, 1951, 1952 **Scottish FA Cup:** 1887, 1902 **Scottish League Cup:** 1972, 1991, 2007 **Second/First Division:** 1894, 1895, 1933, 1981, 1999

INVERNESS CALEDONIAN THISTLE

PLAYERS

MOST APPEARANCES: Ross Tokely (1996-12) 589
MOST GOALS: Dennis Wyness (1999, 00-03, 05-08) 118

Two Highland League clubs – Caledonian and Inverness Thistle – amalgamated to form ICT in 1994 and were elected to the Scottish Third Division. The side worked its way up to the Scottish Premier League for season 2003-04. They had to play at Aberdeen as their ground was then not big enough. They were relegated in 2009 but bounced back for 2010-11.

Founded: 1994
Ground: Caledonian Stadium
Capacity: 7,900
Nickname: ICT, Caley Thistle

HONOURS

First Division: 2004, 2010
Third Division: 1997
Scottish Challenge Cup: 2004

KILMARNOCK

PLAYERS

MOST APPEARANCES: Alan Robertson (1972-89) 607
MOST GOALS: Willie Culley (1911-23) 159

Killie played in the first official football match staged in Scotland, just four years after their formation. They are the country's oldest professional side. Their finest moment, other than winning the league, was when they reached the semi-final of the Inter Cities Fairs Cup (which later became the UEFA Cup) in 1966-67 and were knocked out by Leeds United.

Founded: 1869
Ground: Rugby Park
Capacity: 18,100
Nickname: Killie

HONOURS

League Champions: 1965
First Division: 1898, 1899
Scottish FA Cup: 1920, 1929, 1997

MOTHERWELL

PLAYERS

MOST APPEARANCES: Bob Ferrier (1917-37) 626
MOST LEAGUE GOALS: Hughie Ferguson (1916-25) 284

Motherwell have been ever-present in the Scottish Premier League since its formation in 1998 and have been in Scotand's top-flight since 1984. Record appearance holder Ferrier is also the player to have appeared most times in the Scottish Football League and scored 255 goals for his only professional club. Record scorer Ferguson went on to score 363 goals in total with moves to Cardiff City and Dundee.

Founded: 1886
Ground: Fir Park
Capacity: 13,700
Nickname: Well, Steelmen

HONOURS

League Champions: 1932
First Division: 1954, 1969, 1982, 1985
Scottish FA Cup: 1952, 1991
Scottish League Cup: 1951

ROSS COUNTY

PLAYERS

MOST LEAGUE APPEARANCES:
Mark McCulloch (2002-09) 230
MOST GOALS: Sean Higgins (2002-09) 100

Ross County began life in the Highland Football League, entered the League in 1994 and played for the first time in the Scottish Premier League in 2012-13. They produced a major shock when they reached the Scottish Cup Final in 2010, only to be beaten 3-0 by Dundee United.

Founded: 1929
Ground: Victoria Park
Capacity: 6,300
Nickname: The Staggies

HONOURS

First Division: 2012
Second Division: 2008
Third Division: 1999
Scottish Challenge Cup: 2007, 2011

PLAYERS

MOST APPEARANCES: Alan Main (1995-03, 07-10) 361
MOST GOALS: John Brogan (1976-84) 140

St. Johnstone arrived back in the Scottish Premier League in 2009 after seven years outside of the top-flight. They were founder members of the Premier League in 1997 and hit the heights with a third place finished behind Rangers and Celtic in 1999. They were relegated in 2002.

ST. JOHNSTONE

Founded: 1884
Ground: McDiarmid Park
Capacity: 10,600
Nickname: Saintees

HONOURS

First Division:
1983, 1990, 1997, 2009
Division Two:
1924, 1960. 1963
**Scottish
League Challenge Cup:** 2008

PLAYERS

MOST APPEARANCES: Hugh Murray (1996-12) 462
MOST LEAGUE GOALS: David McCrae (1923-34) 221

Season 1979-80 saw Saints finished behind Aberdeen and Celtic in Scotland's top-flight for their highest-ever finish. In 2001 they lost just one of their games in the Premier League but were still relegated and didn't return until 2006.

ST. MIRREN

Founded: 1977
Ground: New St. Mirren Park
Capacity: 8,000
Nickname: Buddies, Saints

HONOURS

First Division:
1968, 1977, 2000, 2006
Scottish FA Cup:
1926, 1959, 1987
Scottish Challenge Cup: 2005

SCOTTISH LEAGUES 2012-13

Due to Rangers forming a new club, the final shape of the three Scottish divisions had to be changed for 2012-13. The listing below is how the teams **would** have lined up, if the Glasgow giants had been allowed to continue in the SPL.

DIVISION ONE
Cowdenbeath
Dumbarton
Dundee
Dunfermline
Falkirk

Greenock Morton
Hamilton Academical
Livingston
Partick Thistle
Raith Rovers

DIVISION TWO
Airdrie United
Albion Rovers
Alloa Athletic
Arbroath
Ayr United
Brechin City
East Fife
Forfar Athletic
Queen of the South
Stenhousemuir

DIVISION THREE
Annan Athletic
Berwick Rangers
Clyde
East Stirlingshire

Elgin City
Montrose
Peterhead
Queen's Park
Stirling Albion
Stranraer

Dunfermline

SCOTTISH LEAGUES

The Scottish League was founded in 1890 and a second division was formed in 1893.

A third division lasted just two seasons between 1923-25. From 1926-39 there were just two divisions. Three divisions began again in 1946 but went back to two in 1955. They were named Divisions 1 and 2 in 1956. In 1975 a third division was again back in operation.

In 1995 four divisions of ten teams came into operation before the breakaway Scottish Premier League came into existence in 1998.

SCOTTISH LEAGUE

Year	Winner
1891	Dumbarton and Rangers
1892	Dumbarton
1893	Celtic

FIRST DIVISION

Year	Winner
1894	Celtic
1895	Heart of Midlothian
1896	Celtic
1897	Heart of Midlothian
1898	Celtic
1899	Rangers
1900	Rangers
1901	Rangers
1902	Rangers
1903	Hibernian
1904	Third Lanark
1905	Celtic
1906	Celtic
1907	Celtic
1908	Celtic
1909	Celtic
1910	Celtic
1911	Rangers
1912	Rangers
1913	Rangers
1914	Celtic
1915	Celtic
1916	Celtic
1917	Celtic
1918	Rangers
1919	Celtic
1920	Rangers
1921	Rangers
1922	Celtic
1923	Rangers
1924	Rangers
1925	Rangers
1926	Celtic
1927	Rangers
1928	Rangers
1929	Rangers
1930	Rangers
1931	Rangers
1932	Motherwell
1933	Rangers
1934	Rangers
1935	Rangers
1936	Celtic
1937	Rangers
1938	Celtic
1939	Rangers
1939-46	World War II
1947	Rangers
1948	Hibernian
1949	Rangers
1950	Rangers
1951	Hibernian
1952	Hibernian
1953	Rangers
1954	Celtic
1955	Aberdeen
1956	Rangers
1957	Rangers
1958	Heart of Midlothian
1959	Rangers
1960	Heart of Midlothian
1961	Rangers
1962	Dundee
1963	Rangers
1964	Rangers
1965	Kilmarnock
1966	Celtic
1967	Celtic
1968	Celtic
1969	Celtic
1970	Celtic
1971	Celtic
1972	Celtic
1973	Celtic
1974	Celtic
1975	Rangers

PREMIER DIVISION

Year	Winner
1976	Rangers
1977	Celtic
1978	Rangers
1979	Celtic
1980	Aberdeen
1981	Celtic
1982	Celtic
1983	Dundee United
1984	Aberdeen
1985	Aberdeen
1986	Celtic
1987	Rangers
1988	Celtic
1989	Rangers
1990	Rangers
1991	Rangers
1992	Rangers
1993	Rangers
1994	Rangers
1995	Rangers
1996	Rangers
1997	Rangers
1998	Celtic

PREMIER LEAGUE

Year	Winner
1999	Rangers
2000	Rangers
2001	Celtic
2002	Celtic
2003	Rangers
2004	Celtic
2005	Rangers
2006	Celtic
2007	Celtic
2008	Celtic
2009	Rangers
2010	Rangers
2011	Rangers
2012	Celtic

DIVISION TWO

Year	Winner
1894	Hibernian
1895	Hibernian
1896	Abercorn
1897	Partick Thistle
1898	Kilmarnock
1899	Kilmarnock
1900	Partick Thistle
1901	St. Bernard's
1902	Port Glasgow Athletic
1903	Airdrieonians
1904	Hamilton Academical
1905	Clyde
1906	Leith Athletic
1907	St. Bernard's
1908	Raith Rovers
1909	Abercorn
1910	Leith Athletic
1911	Dumbarton
1912	Ayr United
1913	Ayr United

SCOTTISH LEAGUES CONTINUED . . .

1914	Cowdenbeath
1915	Cowdenbeath
1915-21	World War I
1922	Alloa Athletic
1923	Queen's Park
1924	St. Johnstone
1925	Dundee United
1926	Dunfermline Athletic
1927	Bo'ness United
1928	Ayr United
1929	Dundee United
1930	Leith Athletic
1931	Third Lanark
1932	East Stirlingshire
1933	Hibernian
1934	Albion Rovers
1935	Third Lanark
1936	Falkirk
1937	Ayr United
1938	Raith Rovers
1939	Cowdenbeath
1939-46	World War II

B DIVISION

1947	Dundee
1948	East Fife
1949	Raith Rovers
1950	Morton
1951	Queen of the South
1952	Clyde
1953	Stirling Albion
1954	Motherwell
1955	Airdrieonians
1956	Queen's Park

DIVISION TWO

1957	Clyde
1958	Stirling Albion
1959	Ayr United
1960	St. Johnstone
1961	Stirling Albion
1962	Clyde
1963	St. Johnstone
1964	Morton
1965	Stirling Albion
1966	Ayr United
1967	Morton

1968	St. Mirren
1969	Motherwell
1970	Falkirk
1971	Partick Thistle
1972	Dumbarton
1973	Clyde
1974	Airdrieonians
1975	Falkirk

FIRST DIVISION

1976	Partick Thistle
1977	St. Mirren
1978	Morton
1979	Dundee
1980	Heart of Midlothian
1981	Hibernian
1982	Motherwell
1983	St. Johnstone
1984	Morton
1985	Motherwell
1986	Hamilton Academical
1987	Morton
1988	Hamilton Academical
1989	Dunfermline Athletic
1990	St. Johnstone
1991	Falkirk
1992	Dundee
1993	Raith Rovers
1994	Falkirk
1995	Raith Rothers
1996	Dunfermline Athletic
1997	St. Johnstone
1998	Dundee
1999	Hibernian
2000	St. Mirren
2001	Livingston
2002	Partick Thistle
2003	Falkirk
2004	Inverness Caledonian Thistle
2005	Falkirk
2006	St. Mirren
2007	Gretna
2008	Hamilton Academical
2009	St. Johnstone
2010	Inverness Caledonian Thistle

2011	Dunfermline Athletic
2012	Ross County

THIRD DIVISION

1924	Arthurlie
1925	Title not awarded as fixtures not completed

C DIVISION

1947	Stirling Albion
1948	East Stirlingshire
1949	Forfar Athletic
1949-55	Split into north-east and south-west sections
1950	Hibernian A Clyde A
1951	Heart of Midlothian A Clyde A
1952	Dundee A Rangers A
1953	Aberdeen A Rangers A
1954	Brechin City Rangers A
1955	Aberdeen A Partick Thistle A

DIVISION THREE

1995	Forfar Athletic
1996	Livingston
1997	Inverness Caledonian Thistle
1998	Alloa Athletic
1999	Ross County
2000	Queen's Park
2001	Hamilton Academical
2002	Brechin City
2003	Greenock Morton
2004	Stranraer
2005	Gretna
2006	Cowdenbeath
2007	Berwick Rangers
2008	East Fife
2009	Dumbarton
2010	Livingston
2011	Arbroath
2012	Alloa

62 SCOTTISH LEAGUES \\\\\\

CONFERENCE

The Conference is the fifth tier of English football and the first outside of the Football League. The teams are often referred to as non-League, although some sides are full-time.

The Conference was formed in 1979 by teams from the Northern Premier League and Southern League.

In 2004 it also created Conference North and South as feeder divisions for the National competition.

In the past clubs would have to seek election to the Football League – and were quite often refused entry.

Now the Conference winners gain automatic promotion to League Two and a second team goes up through a play-off system.

The two bottom sides in League Two are relegated to the Conference at the end of the season.

ALL THE WINNERS...

1980 Altrincham	**1994** Kidderminster Harriers*	**2004** Chester City	
1981 Altrincham		**2005** Barnet	
1982 Runcorn	**1995** Macclesfield Town*	**2006** Accrington Stanley	
1983 Enfield			
1984 Maidstone United	**1996** Stevenage Borough*	**2007** Dagenham and Redbridge	
1985 Wealdstone			
1986 Enfield	**1997** Macclesfield Town	**2008** Aldershot Town	
1987 Scarborough	**1998** Halifax Town	**2009** Burton Albion	
1988 Lincoln City	**1999** Cheltenham Town	**2010** Stevenage Borough	
1989 Maidstone United	**2000** Kidderminster Harriers		
1990 Darlington		**2011** Crawley Town	
1991 Barnet	**2001** Rushden and Diamonds	**2012** Fleetwood Town	
1992 Colchester United			
1993 Wycombe Wanderers	**2002** Boston United		
	2003 Yeovil Town		

* Were not promoted because their grounds did not meet Football League requirements.

2011

FA TROPHY

The trophy is the FA Cup of non-league football and is competed for from teams from the Conference, Southern, Isthmian and Northern Premier Leagues.

ALL THE WINNERS...

1970 Macclesfield Town	**1984** Northwich Victoria	**1995** Woking	**2008** Ebbsfleet United
1971 Telford United	**1985** Wealdstone	**1996** Macclesfield Town	**2009** Stevenage Borough
1972 Stafford Rangers	**1986** Altrincham	**1997** Woking	
1973 Scarborough	**1987** Kidderminster Harriers	**1998** Cheltenham Town	**2010** Barrow
1974 Morecambe		**1999** Kingstonian	**2011** Darlington
1975 Matlock Town	**1988** Enfield	**2000** Kingstonian	**2012** York City
1976 Scarborough	**1989** Telford United	**2001** Canvey Island	
1977 Scarborough	**1990** Barrow	**2002** Yeovil Town	
1978 Altrincham	**1991** Wycombe Wanderers	**2003** Burscough	
1979 Stafford Rangers		**2004** Hednesford Town	
1980 Dagenham	**1992** Colchester United	**2005** Grays Athletic	
1981 Bishop's Stortford	**1993** Wycombe Wanderers	**2006** Grays Athletic	
1982 Enfield		**2007** Stevenage Borough	
1983 Telford United	**1994** Woking		

2008

AC Milan

Current league: Serie A

Ground: San Siro, 80,000

Nickname: Rossoneri

Famous old boy: Paolo Maldini, defender 1985-2009

CLAIM TO FAME: Serie A 18, Italian Cup 5, European Cup (Champions League) 7, European Super Cup 5, FIFA Club World Cup 1,

Ajax

Current league: Eredivisie

Ground: Amsterdam Arena, 52,300

Nickname: de Godenzone, I Lancieri

Famous old boy: Johan Cruyff, striker 1964-73, 81-83

CLAIM TO FAME: Dutch title 31, Dutch Cup 18, Champions League 4, Cup Winners' Cup 1, UEFA Cup 1.

Anderlecht

Current league: Belgian Pro

Ground: Constant Vanden Stadium, 28,000

Nickname: Purple and white

Famous old boy: Paul van Himst, striker 1960-75

CLAIM TO FAME: Belgian title 30, Belgian Cup 9, League Cup 1, Belgian Super Cup 9, European Cup Winners' Cup 2, UEFA Cup 1, European Super Cup 2.

Anzhi Makhachkala

Current league: Russian Premier

Ground: Dinamo Stadium, 15,200

Nickname: Wild division

Famous old boy: Samuel Eto'o, striker 2011-

CLAIM TO FAME: Anzhi was only formed in 1991 but hit the headlines in January 2011 with a massive take over that led to them signing big name players.

Atletico Madrid

Current league: La Liga
Ground: Vincente Calderon Stadium 54,900
Nickname: Los Colchoneros, Los Indios
Famous old boy: Luis Aragones, striker 1964-1974

CLAIM TO FAME: La Liga 9, Copa del Rey 9,
Spanish Super Cup 1, Europa League 1,
UEFA Super Cup 1, Intercontinental Cup 1.

Barcelona

Current league: La Liga
Ground: Camp Nou, 99,300
Nickname: Barca
Famous old boy: Joseph Guardiola, midfield 1990-2001

CLAIM TO FAME: La Liga 21, Copa del Rey 25,
Spanish Super Cup 10, European Cup 4,
FIFA Club World Cup 2.

Basel

Current league: Swiss Super
Ground: St. Jakob Park, 38,500
Nickname: FFC, Bebbi
Famous old boy: Beni Huggel, midfielder 1998-05,
2007-

CLAIM TO FAME: Swiss League 14, Swiss Cup 10,
League Cup 1.

Bayer Leverkusen

Current league: Bundesliga
Ground: Bay Arena, 30,200
Nickname: Werkself
Famous old boy: Michael Ballack, 199-02, 10-12

CLAIM TO FAME: UEFA Cup 1, League Cup 1,
five times Bundesliga runners-up

Bayern Munich

Current league: Bundesliga

Ground: Allianz Arena, 69,900

Nickname: Bavarians, Reds

Famous old boy: Lothar Matthaus, midfielder 1984-88, 1992-2000

CLAIM TO FAME: German title 22, German Cup 15, League Cup 6, Super Cup 4, European Cup 4, UEFA Cup Winners' Cup 1, UEFA Cup 1.

Benfica

Current league: Primeira League

Ground: Estadio da Luz, 65,600

Nickname: Eagles, Reds

Famous old boy: Joao Pinto, forward, 1992-2000

CLAIM TO FAME: 32 times Portugal champions, Portugal Cup 27, League Cup 3, European Cup 2.

Boca Juniors

Current league: Primera Division

Ground: Estadio Alberton J. Armando, 57,700

Nickname: Genoese, Blue and Gold

Famous old boy: Juan Riquelme, midfielder 1995-02, 2007-

CLAIM TO FAME: Argentina championship 24, Argentina Cup 1.

Borussia Monchengladbach

Current league: Bundesliga

Ground: Borussia Park, 54,000

Nickname: The Foals

Famous old boy: Berti Vogts, defender 1965-79

CLAIM TO FAME: Bundesliga 5, German Cup 3, UEFA Cup 2.

Corinthians

Current league: Brasileiro Serie A

Ground: Parque Sao Jorge, 14,000

Nickname: The People's Club, Almighty

Famous old boy: Carlos Tevez, striker, 2004-06

CLAIM TO FAME: Brasileiro 5, Brazil Cup 3,
Brazil Super Cup 1, State champions 26,
FIFA Club World Cup 1, Atlantic Cup 1.

CSKA Moscow

Current league: Russian Premier

Ground: Arena Khimki, 18,600

Nickname: Horses, Army Men

Famous old boy: Vagner Love, striker 2004-11

CLAIM TO FAME: Premier League 3, Russia/Soviet Cup
11, Russia Super Cup 4, UEFA Cup 1, Soviet League 7.

CSKA Sofia

Current league: Bulgarian A PFG

Ground: Balgarska Armiya Stadium, 22,000

Nickname: Reds, Army Men

Famous old boy: Hristo Stoichkov, striker 1984-90,
1998

CLAIM TO FAME: Bulgaria Champions 31,
Bulgaria Cup 10, Bulgaria Super Cup 4.

Dinamo Zagreb

Current league: Prva HNL

Ground: Stadion Maksimir, 35,800

Nickname: The Blues

Famous old boy: Igor Cvitanovic, striker 1989-97,
99-02

CLAIM TO FAME: Yugosla/Croatian title 18, Cup 19,
Super Cup 4, Inter Cities Fairs Cup 1.

Dynamo Kiev

Current league: Ukrainian Premier

Ground: Lobanovskyi Dynamo Stadium, 16,800

Nickname: White-Blues

Famous old boy: Andriy Shevchenko, striker 1994-99, 2009-

CLAIM TO FAME: Soviet/Ukraine title 26, Cup 18, Super Cup 8, Cup Winners' Cup 2, UEFA Super Cup 2.

Dynamo Moscow

Current league: Russian Premier

Ground: Arena Khimki, 18,600

Nickname: White-blues, Louders, Policemen

Famous old boy: Lev Yashin, keeper, 1950-70

CLAIM TO FAME: Soviet League 11, Soviet Cup 6, Soviet Super Cup 1, Russia Cup 1.

Fenerbahce

Current league: Super Lig

Ground: Sukru Saracoglu Stadium, 50,500

Nickname: Yellow canaries

Famous old boy: Mujdat Yetkiner, midfielder 1980-1995

CLAIM TO FAME: Turkish Champions 18, Turkish Cup 5, Super Cup 8.

Ferencvaros

Current league: OTP Bank Liga

Ground: Stadion Albert Florian, 18,100

Nickname: Green Eagles

Famous old boy: Peter Lipcsei, midfielder 1990-95, 97-98, 00-10

CLAIM TO FAME: Hungarian Champions 28, Hungarian Cup 20, Super Cup 4, Inter Cities Fairs Cup 1.

Feyenoord

Current league: Eredivisie

Ground: Feijenoord Stadium, 51,100

Nickname: Stadiumclub, Club from the South

Famous old boy: Patrick Paauwe, midfielder 1998-2006

CLAIM TO FAME: Dutch title 14, Dutch Cup 11, Intercontinental Cup 1, European Cup 1, UEFA Cup 2.

FC Copenhagen

Current league: Danish Superliga

Ground: Parken, 38,000

Nickname: The Lions

Famous old boy: Christian Lonstrup, midfielder 1992-96, 98-05

CLAIM TO FAME: Danish Superliga 9, Danish Cup 5, League Cup 1, Super Cup 3.

Flamengo

Current league: Brasileiro Serie A

Ground: Engenhao, 46,900

Nickname: Scarlet-black, Vulture

Famous old boy: Junior, midfielder 1974-84, 89-93

CLAIM TO FAME: State champions 32, Brazil Serie A 6, Brazil Cup 2, Champions Cup 1, Copa Libertadores 1, Intercontinental Cup 1.

Galatasaray

Current league: Turkey Super Lig

Ground: Turk Telekom Arena, 52,600

Nickname: Lions, Yellow-reds

Famous old boy: Hakan Sukur, striker 1992-95, 95-00, 03-08

CLAIM TO FAME: Turkish Champions 18, Turkey Cup 14, Super Cup 11, UEFA Super Cup 1, Europa League 1.

Hamburg

Current league: Bundesliga

Ground: Imtech Stadium, 56,800

Nickname: Rothosen, The Dinosaur

Famous old boy: Kevin Keegan, striker 1977-80

CLAIM TO FAME: German Champions 6, German Cup 3, League Cup 2, European Cup 1, UEFA Cup Winners' Cup 1.

Helsingborgs

Current league: Allsvenskan

Ground: Olympia, 17,200

Nickname: The Reds, Milk Cow

Famous old boy: Henrik Larsson, striker 1992-93, 06-09

CLAIM TO FAME: Swedish Champions 5, Allsvenskan 7, Swedish Cup 5, Swedish Super Cup 2.

HJK Helsinki

Current league: Veikkausliiga

Ground: Sonera Stadium, 10,700

Nickname: Klubi

Famous old boy: Antti Niemi, keeper 1991-95

CLAIM TO FAME: Finnish Champions 24, Finnish Cup 11, League Cup 4.

Independiente

Current league: Primera Division

Ground: Estadio Libertadores de America, 44,000

Nickname: The Red, King of Cups

Famous old boy: Ricardo Bochini, midfielder 1971-91

CLAIM TO FAME: Argentina Champions 16, Copa Libertadores 7, South America Super Cup 2, Interamerican Cup, Copa Sudamericana 1, Recopa Sudamericana 1.

Inter Milan

Current league: Serie A

Ground: San Siro, 80,000

Nickname: Nerazzurri, Inter

Famous old boy: Javier Zanetti, defender 1995-

CLAIM TO FAME: Serie A 18, Italian Cup 7, Italian Super Cup 5, Intercontinental Cup 2, FIFA Club World Cup 1, European Cup 3, UEFA Cup 3.

Internacional

Current league: Brasileiro Serie A

Ground: Beira-Rio, 56,000

Nickname: The Red, People's Club

Famous old boy: Edinho, midfielder 2003-08

CLAIM TO FAME: State title 41, Serie A 3, Copa Brasil 1, Copa Libertadores 2, Copa Sudamerica 1, Recopa Sudamerica 2, FIFA Club World Cup 1.

Juventus

Current league: Serie A

Ground: Juventus Stadium, 41,000

Nickname: The Old Lady

Famous old boy: Alessandro del Piero, striker 1993-

CLAIM TO FAME: Italian Champions 28, Italian Cup 9, Italian Super Cup 4, European Cup 2, UEFA Cup Winners' Cup 1, UEFA Cup 3, UEFA Super Cup 2, Intercontinental Cup 2.

Lazio

Current league: Serie A

Ground: Stadio Olimpico, 72,400

Nickname: Eagles, White and blue

Famous old boy: Giuseppe Favalli, defender 1992-04

CLAIM TO FAME: Italian Champions 2, Italian Cup 5, Italian Super Cup 3, UEFA Cup Winners' Cup 1, UEFA Super Cup 1.

Legia Warsaw

Current league: Ekstraklasa

Ground: Polish Army Stadium, 31,000

Nickname: Military, Legionnaires

Famous old boy: Lucjan Brychczy, striker 1954-69

CLAIM TO FAME: Polish Champions 8, Polish Cup 15, Polish Super Cup 4, League Cup 1.

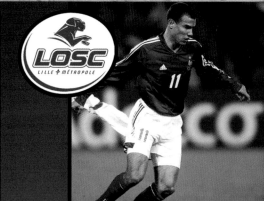

Lille

Current league: Ligue 1

Ground: Stade Lille-Metropole, 18,100

Nickname: Les Dogues

Famous old boy: Bruno Cheyrou, midfielder 1998-02

CLAIM TO FAME: French Champions 3, French Cup 6, Coupe Gambardella 1.

Linfield

Current league: IFA Premiership

Ground: Windsor Park, 24,700

Nickname: The Blues

Famous old boy: Noel Bailie, defender 1989-2011

CLAIM TO FAME: Irish Champions 51, Irish Cup 42, League Cup 9.

Lokomotiv Moscow

Current league: Russian Premier

Ground: Lokomotiv Stadium, 28,800

Nickname: Loko, Red-greens

Famous old boy: Vladimir Maminov, midfielder 1992-2008

CLAIM TO FAME: Russian Champions 2, Russian Cup 5, Russian Super Cup 2, Soviet Cup 2.

Malmo

Current league: Allsvenskan
Ground: Swedbank Stadion, 24,000
Nickname: The Blues
Famous old boy: Bo Larsson, forward 1962-66, 69-79

CLAIM TO FAME: Swedish Champions 16, Allsvenskan 19, Swedish Cup 14.

Maribor

Current league: Slovenia PRVA
Ground: Ljudski vrt, 12,900
Nickname: The Purples, The Voice
Famous old boy: Gregor Zidan, midfielder, 1993-01
CLAIM TO FAME: Slovenia Champions 10, Slovenia Cup 6, Slovenia Super Cup 1.

Monaco

Current league: Ligue 2
Ground: Stade Louis II, 18,500
Nickname: Red and Whites
Famous old boy: Youri Djorkaeff, striker 1990-95

CLAIM TO FAME: French Champions 7, French Cup 4, League Cup 1, Trophy of Champions 4.

Olympiacos

Current league: Greek Super League
Ground: Karaiskakis Stadium, 32,100
Nickname: The Legend, Red-whites
Famous old boy: Predrag Dordevic, midfielder 1996-2009

CLAIM TO FAME: Greek Champions 39, Greek Cup 25, Greek Super Cup 4, Greater Greece Cup 2.

Olympique Lyonnais

Current league: Ligue 1
Ground: Stade de Gerland, 40,500
Nickname: The Kids
Famous old boy: Serge Chiesa, midfielder 1969-83

CLAIM TO FAME: French Champions 7, French Cup 5, League Cup 1, Trophee des Champions 7.

Olympique Marseille

Current league: Ligue 1
Ground: Stade Velodrome, 60,000
Nickname: Les Phoceens
Famous old boy: Jean-Pierre Papin, striker 1986-92

CLAIM TO FAME: French Champions 9, French Cup 10, League Cup 3, Trophee des Champions 3, European Cup 1.

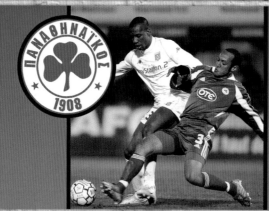

Panathinaikos

Current league: Greek Super League
Ground: Olympic Stadium, 69,600
Nickname: Shamrock, Greens
Famous old boy: Mimis Domazos, midfielder 1959-78, 1980

CLAIM TO FAME: Greek Champions 20, Greek Cup 17, Greek Super Cup 4, Greater Greece Cup 1.

Paris Saint German

Current league: Ligue 1
Ground: Parc des Princes, 48,700
Nickname: Les Parisiens, Les Rouge-et-Bleu
Famous old boy: Pauleta, striker 2003-08

CLAIM TO FAME: French Champions 2, French Cup 8, League Cup 3, Trophee des Champions 2, UEFA Cup Winners' Cup 1.

Partizan

Current league: Serbian Super Liga

Ground: Stadion FK Partizan, 32,700

Nickname: Black and Whites, Steamroller

Famous old boy: Mom ilo Vukoti , midfielder 1968-78, 79-84

CLAIM TO FAME: Yugoslav title 11, Yugoslavia, Serbia and Montenegro title 8, Serbia title 4, Yugoslav Cup 5, FR Yugoslav Cup 4, Serbia Cup 3.

Porto

Current league: Primeira Liga

Ground: Estadio do Dragao, 50,400

Nickname: Dragons, Portistas

Famous old boy: Joao Pinto, defender 1981-97

CLAIM TO FAME: Portugal title 26, Portugal Cup 20, Portugal Super Cup 18, European Cup 2, Europa League 2, UEFA Super Cup 1, Intercontinental Cup 2.

PSV Eindhoven

Current league: Eredivisie

Ground: Philips Stadium, 35,000

Nickname: Peasants, Red white army

Famous old boy: Willy van der Kuylen, midfielder 1964-81

CLAIM TO FAME: Dutch Champions 21, Dutch Cup 9, European Cup 1, UEFA Cup 1.

Real Madrid

Current league: La Liga

Ground: Estadio Santiago Bernabeu, 85,400

Nickname: The Whites, Vinkings

Famous old boy: Raul, striker 1994-2010

CLAIM TO FAME: Spanish title 32, Copa del Rey 18, Spain Super Cup 8, League Cup 1, European Cup 9, UEFA Cup 2, UEFA Super Cup 1, Intercontinental Cup 3.

Roma

Current league: Serie A

Ground: Stadio Olimpico, 72,700

Nickname: Wolves, Yellow-reds

Famous old boy: Franceso Totti, striker, 1992-

CLAIM TO FAME: Italian Champions 3, Italian Cup 9, Italian Super Cup 2, Inter Cities Fairs Cup 1.

Rosenborg

Current league: Tippeligaen

Ground: Lerkendal Stadion, 21,100

Nickname: Troillongan

Famous old boy: Roar Strand, midfielder 1989-201

CLAIM TO FAME: Norway Champions 22, Norway Cup 9, Super Cup 1.

Santos

Current league: Brasileiro Serie A

Ground: Vila Belmiro, 15,800

Nickname: Santastico, Fish

Famous old boy: Pele, forward 1956-74

CLAIM TO FAME: Brazil Champions 8, Paulista 20, Brazil Cup 1, Copa Libertadores 3, CONMEBOL Cup 1, Intercontinental cup 2, Recopa Sudamericana 1, Intercontinental Super Cup 1.

Sao Paulo

Current league: Brasileiro Serie A

Ground: Morumbi, 67,400

Nickname: Sovereign, The Dearest

Famous old boy: Rogerio Ceni, keeper 1992-

CLAIM TO FAME: Brazil Champions 6, Paulista 21, Copa Libertadores 3, CONMEBOL Cup 1, Recopa Sudamericana 2, Supercopa Sudamericana 1, FIFA Club World Cup 1, Intercontinental Cup 1.

Schalke 04

Current league: Bundesliga
Ground: Veltins Arena, 61,600
Nickname: Royal Blues, Miners
Famous old boy: Klaus Fischer, striker 1970-81

CLAIM TO FAME: German Champions 7, German Cup 5, German Super Cup 1, League Cup 1, UEFA Cup 1.

Shakhtar Donetsk

Current league: Ukrainian Premier
Ground: Donbass Arena, 52,500
Nickname: Miners, Moles
Famous old boy: Andriy Vorobey, striker 1997-2007

CLAIM TO FAME: Ukraine Champions 7, Ukraine Cup 8, Ukraine Super Cup 3, Soviet Cup 4, Soviet Super Cup 1, UEFA Cup 1.

Shamrock Rovers

Current league: League of Ireland Premier
Ground: Tallaght Stadium, 6,000
Nickname: Hoops, Rovers
Famous old boy: Derek Tracey, midfielder 1989-2006

CLAIM TO FAME: Irish Champions 17, Irish Cup 24, Irish Shield 18, League Cup 1.

Sparta Prague

Current league: Gambrinus Liga
Ground: Generali Arena, 20,800
Nickname: Iron Sparta, Reds
Famous old boy: Pavel Nedved, midfielder 1992-96

CLAIM TO FAME: Czech Republic Champions 11, Czech Champions 24, Czech Cup 5, Czech Super Cup 1, Czechoslovak Cup 12.

Spartak Moscow

Current league: Russian Premier
Ground: Luzhniki Stadium, 78,300
Nickname: The people's club
Famous old boy: Yegot Titov, midfielder 1995-2008

CLAIM TO FAME: Russian Champions 9, Russian Cup 3, Soviet Champions 12, Soviet Cup 10.

Sporting Lisbon

Current league: Primeira Liga
Ground: Estadio Jose Alvalade, 50,000
Nickname: Lions
Famous old boy: Liedson, striker, 2003-11

CLAIM TO FAME: Portugal Champions 18, Portugal Cup 19, Portugal Super Cup 7, UEFA Cup Winners' Cup 1.

Valencia

Current league: La Liga
Ground: Estadio Mestalla, 55,000
Nickname: The Orange
Famous old boy: David Villa, striker 2005-10

CLAIM TO FAME: Spanish Champions 6, Copa del Rey 7, Spanish Super Cup 1, UEFA Cup Winners' Cup 1, UEFA Cup 1, Inter Cities Fairs Cup 2, UEFA Super Cup 2.

Zenit St. Petersburg

Current league: Russian Premier
Ground: Petrovsky Stadium, 21,400
Nickname: Bags, blue white-light blue
Famous old boy: Lev Burchalkin, striker 1957-72

CLAIM TO FAME: Russia Champions 2, Russia Cup 2, Russian Premier League Cup 1, Russian Super Cup 1, Soviet Champions 1, Soviet Cup 1, Soviet Super Cup 1, UEFA Cup 1, UEFA Super Cup 1.

THE
PLAYERS

YOUR **A-Z GUIDE** OF CURRENT STARS AND **LEGENDS** OF THE **BEAUTIFUL** GAME

SERGIO **AGUERO**

Position: Striker
Birth date: June 2, 1988
Birth place: Quilmes, Argentina
Height: 1.73m (5ft 8in)
Clubs: Independiente, Atletico Madrid, Manchester City
International: Argentina
Began senior career: 2003
It's a fact: City forked out a staggering £38m to buy Aguero from Atletico in summer 2011, heading off interest from Chelsea, Manchester United and Real Madrid. The striker hit 30 goals in his first 48 games for the Citizens, won the Premier League and was the Etihad Player of the Year.

XABI **ALONSO**

Position: Midfielder
Birth date: November 25, 1981
Birth place: Tolosa, Spain
Height: 1.83m (6ft)
Clubs: Real Sociedad, Eibar (loan), Liverpool, Real Madrid
International: Spain
Began senior career: 1999
It's a fact: Alonso signed for Liverpool in a £10m deal in 2004. He won the European Cup in his first season, followed by the European Super Cup, FA Cup and Charity Shield. Joined Real Madrid for £30m in 2009. Reached the 100-cap mark for his country during Euro 2012.

BENOIT **ASSOU-EKOTTO**

Position: Defender
Birth date: March 24, 1984
Birth place: Arras, France
Height: 1.78m (5ft 10in)
Clubs: Lens, Tottenham
International: Cameroon
Began senior career: 2004
It's a fact: Assou-Ekotto signed for Spurs for around £3.5m in 2006 when Martin Jol was still manager at White Hart Lane. The left back steadily improved his form to become a regular in the first-team whilst Harry Redknapp was in charge at Tottenham.

DEMBA **BA**

Position: Striker
Birth date: May 25, 1985
Birth place: Sevres, France
Height: 1.89m (6ft 2in)
Clubs: Rouen, Mouscron, Hoffenheim, West Ham, Newcastle.
International: Senegal
Began senior career: 2005
It's a fact: Stoke were going to buy Ba for £7m from Hoffenheim but turned down the deal when he failed a medical. He played 12 games at West Ham but when the Hammers were relegated Newcastle got him on a free transfer.

LEIGHTON **BAINES**

Everton

Position: Defender
Birth date: Dec 11, 1984
Birth place: Kirkby, Merseyside
Height: 1.7m (5ft 7in)
Clubs: Wigan, Everton
International: England
Began senior career: 2002
It's a fact: The full back was on the books at Goodison Park as a youngster but moved on to sign for Wigan Athletic when he was 17. He returned to Everton in 2007 when he cost the Toffees £6m. He has twice been Everton's Players' Player of the Season and once the club's Player of the Season.

GARETH **BALE**

TOTTENHAM HOTSPUR

Position: Winger
Birth date: July 16, 1989
Birth place: Cardiff, Wales
Height: 1.83m (6ft)
Clubs: Southampton, Tottenham
International: Wales
Began senior career: 2006
It's a fact: Bale was voted 2011 PFA Player of the Year. He joined Tottenham from Southampton in 2007 for a transfer fee that eventually reached £7m. He had been the Saints' second-youngest player ever, having made his debut at the age of 16 years and 275 days.

MARIO **BALOTELLI**

M.C.F.C.

Position: Striker
Birth date: August 12, 1990
Birth place: Palermo, Italy
Height: 1.88m (6ft 2in)
Clubs: Lumezzane, Inter Milan, Manchester City
International: Italy
Began senior career: 2005
It's a fact: Roberto Mancini, who had been his manager at Inter, paid £24m to his former club to buy Balotelli, after he took over as boss of Manchester City. His 23 Premier League games in 2011-12 produced 13 goals as City won the title.

GARETH **BARRY**

M.C.F.C.

Position: Midfielder
Birth date: Feb 23, 1981
Birth place: Hastings, East Sussex
Height: 1.83m (6ft)
Clubs: Aston Villa, Manchester City
International: England
Began senior career: 1997
It's a fact: A former Under-21 player, Barry made his first full appearance for England back in 2000 when Kevin Keegan was manager. He has been selected by every Three Lions boss since then and has also acted as captain of the side.

DARREN **BENT**

Position: Striker
Birth date: Feb 6, 1984
Birth place:
Tooting, South London
Height: 1.8m (5ft 11in)
Clubs: Ipswich, Charlton, Tottenham, Sunderland, Aston Villa
International: England
Began senior career: 2001
It's a fact: When Bent missed a sitter against Portsmouth, Spurs boss Harry Redknapp said his wife could have scored from the chance! The striker cost Villa an initial £18m when he moved from Sunderland in January 2011.

DIMITAR **BERBATOV**

Position: Striker
Birth date: Jan 30, 1981
Birth place: Blagoevgrad, Bulgaria
Height: 1.89m (6ft 2in)
Clubs: Pirin Blagoevgrad, CSKA Sofia, Bayer Leverkusen,
Tottenham, Manchester United
International: Bulgaria
Began senior career: 1998
It's a fact: Berba improved his English by watching old fashioned gangster movies. He won 77 caps and scored 48 goals for Bulgaria before quitting international football in 2010. He has said he might come out of retirement.

YOHAN **CABAYE**

Position: Midfielder
Birth date: January 14, 1986
Birth place: Tourcoing, France
Height: 1.75m (5ft 9in)
Clubs: Lille, Newcastle United
International: France
Began senior career: 2004
It's a fact: Cabaye helped Lille to win a league and cup double before he left France to play in the Premier League. Newcastle United paid just £4.5m for the player whose form was so impressive that he earned a call-up to France's Euro 2012 squad.

GARY **CAHILL**

Position: Defender
Birth date: December 19, 1985
Birth place: Sheffield
Height: 1.88m (6ft 2in)
Club: Aston Villa, Burnley (loan), Sheffield United (loan), Bolton. Chelsea
International: England
Began senior career: 2004
It's a fact: Having an Irish grandparent meant Cahill could have played for either the Republic or England. He missed out on the Three Lions' Euro 2012 squad due to injury. He joined Chelsea from Bolton for £7m in January 2012 and by the end of the season had won a Champions League winners' medal.

MICHAEL **CARRICK**

Position: Midfielder
Birth date: July 28, 1981
Birth place: Wallsend, Tyneside
Height: 1.83m (6ft)
Clubs: West Ham, Swindon (loan), Birmingham City (loan), Tottenham, Manchester United
International: England
Began senior career: 1998
It's a fact: Carrick has played more than 40 games a season since arriving at Old Trafford from Tottenham for £18m in summer 2006. He has now won four Premier League titles, a League Cup, European Cup and Club World Cup.

ANDY **CARROLL**

Position: Striker
Birth date: Jan 6, 1989
Birth place: Gateshead, Tyne Wear
Height: 1.91 (6ft 3in)
Clubs: Newcastle United, Preston North End (loan), Liverpool
International: England
Began senior career: 2006
It's a fact: Newcastle's youngest player in Europe when he appeared against Palermo in 2006. Part of Newcastle's Championship-winning side in 2010. Joined Liverpool for £35m in January 2011. Has now won a League Cup.

IKER **CASILLAS**

Position: Keeper
Birth date: May 20, 1981
Birth place: Madrid, Spain
Height: 1.82m (6ft)
Clubs: Real Madrid
International: Spain
Began senior career: 1998
It's a fact: The shot-stopper has now played more than 600 games for Real Madrid. Casillas is Spain's record appearance maker with over 130 games. He captained Spain to the 2010 World Cup and the European Championships in 2008 and 2012.

PETR **CECH**

Position: Keeper
Birth date: May 20, 1982
Birth place: Plzen, Czechoslovakia
Height: 1.96m (6ft 5in)
Clubs: Chmel Blsany, Sparta Prague, Rennes, Chelsea
International: Czech Republic
Began senior career: 1999
It's a fact: Cech wears protective head gear following an injury he suffered at Reading in 2006, and which doctors said could have cost him his life. Chelsea paid Rennes £7m for the keeper in summer 2004. He has won three Premier League titles, four FA Cups, two League Cups and a European Cup.

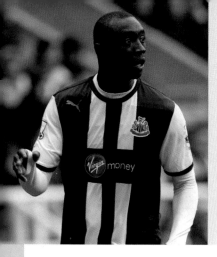

PAPISS **CISSE**

Position: Striker
Birth date: June 3, 1985
Birth place: Dakar, Senegal
Height: 1.83m (6ft)
Clubs: Douanes Dakar, Metz, Cherbourg (loan), Chateauroux (loan), Freiburg, Newcastle United
International: Senegal
Began senior career: 2003
It's a fact: Cisse joined Newcastle for £9m in January 2012 and set a Premier League record with 13 goals in his first 12 games. He already created a new best for an African player in the Bundesliga with 22 goals in 2010-11.

GAEL **CLICHY**

Position: Defender
Birth date: July 25, 1985
Birth place: Toulouse, France
Height: 1.76m (5ft 9in)
Clubs: Cannes, Arsenal, Manchester City
International: France
Began senior career: 2002
It's a fact: When Clichy won the Premier League with Arsenal in 2004 he became the youngest player ever to do so at the age of 18 years and 10 months. He picked up his second league title in 2012 following his £7m move to Manchester City in summer 2011.

ASHLEY **COLE**

Position: Defender
Birth date: December 20, 1980
Birth place: Stepney, East London
Height: 1.76m (5ft 9in)
Clubs: Arsenal, Crystal Palace (loan), Chelsea
International: England
Began senior career: 1998
It's a fact: When he hangs up his boots, Cole fancies going into the music business and has already had discussions with Jay-Z. Has won a record seven FA Cups plus two Premier League titles with Arsenal and one at Chelsea. Cole also has European Cup and League Cup winners' medals.

FABRICIO **COLOCCINI**

Position: Defender
Birth date: January 22, 1982
Birth place: Cordoba, Argentina
Height: 1.83m (6ft)
Clubs: Boca Juniors, AC Milan, San Lorenzo (loan), Alaves (loan), Atletico Madrid (loan), Deportivo, Newcastle United
International: Argentina
Began senior career: 1998
It's a fact: The £10m central defender was appointed Newcastle captain in summer 2011. He won an Olympic Gold medal with Argentina in 2004.

DAVID **DE GEA**

Position: Keeper
Birth date: November 7, 1990
Birth place: Madrid
Height: 1.93m (6ft 4in)
Clubs: Atletico Madrid, Manchester United
International: Spain
Began senior career: 2008
It's a fact: Old Trafford boss Sir Alex Ferguson forked out £18m to Atletico Madrid make Spain Under-21 keeper De Gea a United player in summer 2011. He won the Europa League and UEFA Super Cup with Atletico and his first trophy with United was the Community Shield.

NIGEL **DE JONG**

Position: Midfielder
Birth date: Nov 30, 1984
Birth place: Amsterdam, Holland
Height: 1.74m (5ft 8in)
Clubs: Ajax, Hamburg, Manchester City
International: Holland
Began senior career: 2002
It's a fact: De Jong admits he was lucky to just receive a yellow card for his tackle on Spain's Xabi Alonso in the 2010 World Cup Final. He won the Eredivisie and Dutch Cup with Ajax and has won the Premier League and FA Cup with Man City, who he joined from Hamburg in 2009 for £18m.

CLINT **DEMPSEY**

Position: Striker-midfielder
Birth date: March 9, 1983
Birth place: Nacogdoches, Texas
Height: 1.85m (6ft 1in)
Club: New England Revolution, Fulham
International: USA
Began senior career: 2004
It's a fact: Dempsey is the most prolific American-born goalscorer to appear in England's top-flight. He joined Fulham in 2007 and is the Cottagers' top scorer in the Premier League with 50 goals in 184 appearances to the end of season 2011-12.

ANGEL **DI MARIA**

Position: Winger
Birth date: February 14, 1988
Birth place: Rosario, Argentina
Height: 1.8m (5ft 11in)
Clubs: Rosario Central, Benfica, Real Madrid
International: Argentina
Began senior career: 2005
It's a fact: Nicknamed 'Noodle', Di Maria joined Madrid for £21m in summer 2010. He won the Portuguese League and Portugal Cup with Benfica and added a La Liga title and Copa del Rey with Real Madrid.

STEWART **DOWNING**

Position: Winger
Birth date: July 22, 1984
Birth place: Middlesbrough
Height: 1.8m (5ft 11in)
Clubs: Middlesbrough, Sunderland (loan), Aston Villa, Liverpool
International: England
Began senior career: 2001
It's a fact: Local lad Downing was Middlesbrough's longest-serving player when he left them in 2009, having been with the club for eight years. Villa bought him for £12m. The Villans' Player of the Year was sold to Liverpool in summer 2011 for £20m.

DIDIER **DROGBA**

Position: Striker
Birth date: March 11, 1978
Birth place: Abidjan, Ivory Coast
Height: 1.89m (6ft 2in)
Clubs: Le Mans, Guingamp, Marseille, Chelsea, Shanghai Shenhua
International: Ivory Coast
Began senior career: 1998
It's a fact: The Drog cost Chelsea £24m when they signed him in 2004. He is their fourth-highest goal scorer of all-time. Drogba's last game for Chelsea was the 2012 Champions League Final against Bayern Munich when he scored an equaliser and then the decisive spot-kick in a penalty shoot-out.

EDIN **DZEKO**

Position: Striker
Birth date: March 17, 1986
Birth place: Sarajevo, Bosnia
Height: 1.93m (6ft 4in)
Clubs: Zeljeznicar, Teplice, Usti nad Labem (loan), Wolfsburg, Manchester City
International: Bosnia
Began senior career: 2003
It's a fact: Dzeko was Wolfsburg's record scorer with 59 goals in just 96 games before moving to Manchester City for £27m in January 2011. He hit 21 goals in his first 44 international appearances, leaving him just one short of Bosnia's best.

JOSE **ENRIQUE**

Position: Defender
Birth date: Jan 25, 1986
Birth place: Valencia, Spain
Height: 1.84m (6ft)
Clubs: Levante, Valencia, Celta Vigo (loan), Villarreal, Newcastle United, Liverpool
International: Spain
Began senior career: 2004
It's a fact: Left-back Enrique cost Newcastle around £6m in August 2007 and moved to Liverpool in August 2011 for £5m, shortly before his contract ran out at St. James' Park.

MICHAEL **ESSIEN**

Position: Midfielder
Birth date: Dec 3, 1982
Birth place: Accra, Ghana
Height: 1.78m (5ft 10in)
Clubs: Bastia, Lyon, Chelsea
International: Ghana
Began senior career: 2000
It's a fact: When he joined Chelsea in 2005, Essien was the Blues' record buy and Africa's most expensive footballer at £24.4m. He twice won Ligue 1 with Lyon and then two Premier Leagues, four FA Cups, a League Cup and Champions League with Chelsea.

SAMUEL **ETO'O**

Position: Striker
Birth date: March 10, 1981
Birth place: Nkon, Cameroon
Height: 1.8m (5ft 11in)
Clubs: Real Madrid, Leganes (loan), Espanyol (loan), Mallorca, Barcelona, Inter Milan, Anzhi Makhachkala
International: Cameroon
Began senior career: 1997
It's a fact: The hitman has been African Player of the Year on four occasions, 2003, 2004, 2005 and 2010. Russian side Anzhi signed him in August 2011 and are said to have made him the world's highest-paid player.

PATRICE **EVRA**

Position: Defender
Birth date: May 15, 1981
Birth place: Dakar, Senegal
Height: 1.73m (5ft 8in)
Clubs: Marsala, Monza, Nice, Monaco, Man United
International: France
Began senior career: 1998
It's a fact: The left-back moved to France from Senegal when he was just one-year-old and made his senior debut for Les Bleus in 2004. He has won four Premier League titles, three FA Cups and a European Cup with United. Evra had previously lifted the French League Cup with Monaco.

CESC **FABREGAS**

Position: Midfielder
Birth date: May 4, 1987
Birth place: Vilassar de Mar, Spain
Height: 1.75m (5ft 9in)
Club: Arsenal, Barcelona
International: Spain
Began senior career: 2003
It's a fact: The Gunners got Fabregas from Barca's academy when he was just 16 – and sold him back eight years later for a fee that could reach £33m. He was part of Spain's side that won the 2010 World Cup and European Championships in 2008 and 2012.

DARREN **FLETCHER**

Position: Midfielder
Birth date: Feb 1, 1984
Birth place: Dalkeith, Scotland
Height: 1.84m (6ft)
Club: Manchester United
International: Scotland
Began senior career: 2002
It's a fact: The Scotland captain had to take an "indefinite" break from football just before the start of 2012 because of a bowel illness. Fletcher has four Premier League titles, an FA Cup, two League Cups, a European Cup and Club World Cup to his name.

BRAD **FRIEDEL**

Position: Keeper
Birth date: May 18, 1971
Birth place: Lakewood, USA
Height: 1.88m (6ft 2in)
Clubs: Brondby (loan), Galatasaray, Columbus Crew, Liverpool, Blackburn, Aston Villa, Tottenham
International: USA
Began senior career: 1994
It's a fact: Friedel is the oldest player to appear in the Premier League for both Aston Villa and Tottenham. He earned 82 USA caps from 1992 to 2005. Friedel won the Turkish Cup with Galatasaray and League Cup with Blackburn.

STEVEN **GERRARD**

Position: Midfielder
Birth date: May 30, 1989
Birth place: Whiston, Merseyside
Height: 1.83m (6ft)
Clubs: Liverpool
International: England
Began senior career: 1998
It's a fact: Having signed a new contract in 2012 and agreed at the same time to become a Liverpool FC ambassador when he retires, Gerrard will become a one-club player. Two FA Cups, three League Cups, a European Cup, a UEFA Cup and UEFA Super Cup are among his honours.

SHAY **GIVEN**

Position: Keeper
Birth date: April 20, 1976
Birth place: Lifford, Donegal
Height: 1.85m (6ft 1in)
Clubs: Blackburn, Swindon (loan), Sunderland (loan), Newcastle United, Manchester City, Aston Villa
International: Republic of Ireland
Began senior career: 1994
It's a fact: Given has made a record number of appearances for the Republic and was between the sticks at Newcastle for 463 games. Picked up an FA Cup medal with Man City, as an unused sub at the final.

JOE **HART**

Position: Keeper
Birth date: April 19, 1987
Birth place: Shrewsbury, Shropshire
Height: 1.96m (6ft 5in)
Clubs: Shrewsbury, Manchester City, Tranmere (loan), Blackpool (loan), Birmingham City (loan)
International: England
Began senior career: 2003
It's a fact: Hart won the Premier League Golden Glove for keeping the most clean sheets in both 2010-11 and 2011-12. A Premier League and FA Cup winner with Man City. Birmingham's 2010 Player of the Year.

EDEN **HAZARD**

Position: Midfielder
Birth date: January 7, 1991
Birth place: La Louviere, Belgium
Height: 1.72m (5ft 8in)
Clubs: Lille, Chelsea
International: Belgium
Began senior career: 2007
It's a fact: Hazard's mother, father and younger brother have all played football for their country. Won a league and cup double with Lille in 2010-11. Joined Chelsea in summer 2012 for a fee of around £32m. He was 49 days off his 18th birthday when he made his international debut.

JORDAN **HENDERSON**

Position: Midfielder
Birth date: June 17, 1990
Birth place: Sunderland
Height: 1.82m (6ft)
Clubs: Sunderland, Coventry (loan), Liverpool
International: England
Began senior career: 2008
It's a fact: Sunderland received a staggering £18m from Liverpool for Henderson in summer 2011 after he had played just 79 first-team games. He had just been named the Black Cats' Young Player of the Season for a second successive year.

JAVIER **HERNANDEZ**

Position: Striker
Birth date: June 1, 1988
Birth place: Guadalajara, Mexico
Height: 1.75m (5ft 9in)
Clubs: Guadalajara, Manchester United
International: Mexico
Began senior career: 2006
It's a fact: The Mexican's debut season for United in 2010-11 produced 20 goals in 45 games, 13 of them in the Premier League as the Red Devils won the title. Hernandez, nicknamed Chicharito, had already won Mexico's league.

GONZALO **HIGUAIN**

Position: Striker
Birth date: December 10, 1987
Birth place: Brest, France
Height: 1.84m (6ft)
Clubs: River Plate, Real Madrid
International: Argentina
Began senior career: 2004
It's a fact: His father Jorge was a defender with River Plate and his brother Federico is a forward in Argentine football. He has won three La Liga titles with Madrid plus a Copa del Rey and the Spanish Super Cup. Has played more than 200 games for the club since joining them in 2007.

KEISUKE **HONDA**

Position: Midfielder
Birth date: June 13, 1986
Birth place: Settsu, Japan
Height: 1.82m (5ft 11in)
Clubs: Gamba Osaka, Nagoya Grampus, Venlo, CSKA Moscow
International: Japan
Began senior career: 2005
It's a fact: Honda scored the winner against Cameroon in his country's opening game at World Cup 2010, and then from a free-kick against Denmark. He won the Asian Cup with Japan; Dutch first division at Venlo; and the Russian Cup with CSKA.

TIM **HOWARD**

Everton

Position: Keeper
Birth date: March 6, 1979
Birth place: New Jersey, USA
Height: 1.91m (6ft 3in)
Club: North Jersey Imperials, MetroStars, Manchester United, Everton
International: USA
Began senior career: 1997
It's a fact: Howard started 2012 with a goal against Bolton! His clearance was caught by the wind and went over his opposite number. Everton lost 2-1. He did not miss a league game for Everton from 2008-09 to 2011-12.

ZLATAN **IBRAHIMOVIC**

Position: Striker
Birth date: October 3, 1981
Birth place: Malmo, Sweden
Height: 1.95m (6ft 5in)
Clubs: Malmo, Ajax, Juventus, Inter Milan, Barcelona, AC Milan, PSG
International: Sweden
Began senior career: 1999
It's a fact: When he joined Barcelona in 2009, his contract had a buyout clause of £216m. Barca had bought Ibrahimovic from Inter Milan for £57m but after one season sold him to AC Milan for £22m. Has won the league titles in Holland, Italy and Spain.

ANDRES **INIESTA**

Position: Midfielder
Birth date: May 11, 1984
Birth place: Albacete, Spain
Height: 1.7m (5ft 6in)
Clubs: Barcelona
International: Spain
Began senior career: 2000
It's a fact: Iniesta scored the only goal of the 2010 World Cup Final to give his country extra-time victory over Holland. Also won Euro 2008 and 2012 with Spain. Has won five La Liga titles, two Copa del Rey, five Spanish Super Cups, three European Cups, two UEFA Super Cups and two Club World Cups.

NIKICA **JELAVIC**

Position: Striker
Birth date: August 27, 1986
Birth place: Capljina, Yugoslavia
Height: 1.87m (6ft 2in)
Clubs: Hajduk Split, Zulte Waregem, Rapid Vienna, Rangers, Everton
International: Croatia
Began senior career: 2002
It's a fact: Jelavic signed for Rangers in a £4m transfer in 2010. In the January 2012 transfer window he moved to Everton for £5m and he became the quickest player to reach ten goals for the club. Won the Scottish Premier League and Scottish League Cup in 2010-11.

PETR **JIRACEK**

Position: Midfielder
Birth date: March 2, 1986
Birth place: Tuchonce, Czechoslovakia
Height: 1.8m (5ft 11in)
Clubs: Banik Sokolov, Viktoria Plzen, Wolfsburg
International: Czech Republic
Began senior career: 2006
It's a fact: Won the Czech title, Cup and Super Cup with Viktoria Plzen. Moved to Wolfsburg in December 2011 for around £2.5m. Helped his national side to the quarter-finals of Euro 2012 with a goal against joint hosts Poland.

GLEN **JOHNSON**

Position: Defender
Birth date: August 23, 1984
Birth place: Greenwich, South London
Height: 1.82m (5ft 11in)
Clubs: West Ham United, Millwall (loan), Chelsea, Portsmouth, Liverpool
International: England
Began senior career: 2002
It's a fact: Johnson helped Chelsea to the club's first Premier League title and added a League Cup victory. He won the FA Cup with Portsmouth and then the 2012 League Cup with Liverpool. Bought by Chelsea for £6m, he was sold to Portsmouth for £4m and then to Liverpool for around £17m.

PHIL **JONES**

Position: Defender
Birth date: February 21, 1992
Birth place: Preston, Lancashire
Height: 1.8m (5ft 11in)
Clubs: Blackburn Rovers, Manchester United
International: England
Began senior career: 2009
It's a fact: United handed Jones a five-year contract after signing him from Blackburn for around £16.5m in summer 2011. He made 40 appearances in two seasons for Rovers — and turned out 41 times for the Red Devils in his first season with the Old Trafford side, and won an England call-up.

KAKA

Position: Midfielder
Birth date: April 22, 1982
Birth place: Brasilia, Brazil
Height: 1.83m (6ft)
Clubs: Sao Paulo, AC Milan, Real Madrid
International: Brazil
Began senior career: 2001
It's a fact: Kaka is a devout Christian and celebrates scoring by pointing his finger towards the heavens. He won Serie A, the Italian Super Cup, European Cup, two UEFA Super Cups and a Club World Cup at Milan. He has won La Liga with Madrid plus a Copa del Rey. Kaka won the 2002 World Cup.

VINCENT **KOMPANY**

Position: Defender
Birth date: April 10, 1986
Birth place: Uccle, Belgium
Height: 1.93m (6ft 4in)
Clubs: Anderlecht, Hamburg, Manchester City
International: Belgium
Began senior career: 2003
It's a fact: Kompany cost City £6m from Hamburg in 2008. He captained them to the 2012 Premier League, their first title in 44 years. He twice won the Belgian League with Anderlecht. Kompany was a double Belgian Young Player of the Year and the 2012 Premier League Player of the Year.

DIRK **KUYT**

Position: Striker
Birth date: July 22, 1980
Birth place: Katwijk, Holland
Height: 1.83m (6ft)
Clubs: Quick Boys, Utrecht, Feyenoord, Liverpool, Fenerbahce
International: Holland
Began senior career: 1998
It's a fact: Kuyt lifted the Dutch Cup with Utrecht. The former Dutch Footballer of the Year joined Liverpool for £10m in 2006 and won one League Cup. He was a beaten World Cup finalist with Holland, and with Liverpool lost in the finals of both an FA Cup and the Champions League.

FRANK **LAMPARD**

Position: Midfielder
Birth date: June 20, 1978
Birth place: Romford, Essex
Height: 1.84m (6ft)
Clubs: West Ham, Swansea City (loan), Chelsea
International: England
Began senior career: 1995
It's a fact: Lamps is the highest scoring midfielder in the Premier League. Cost Chelsea £11m in 2001 and has since won three Premier Leagues, four FA Cups, two League Cups and the 2012 Champions League. England Player of the Year in 2004 and 2005 and FWA Footballer of the Year 2005.

SEBASTIAN **LARSSON**

Position: Midfielder
Birth date: June 6, 1985
Birth place: Eskilstuna, Sweden
Height: 1.78m (5ft 10in)
Clubs: Arsenal, Birmingham City, Sunderland
International: Sweden
Began senior career: 2004
It's a fact: Larsson won the 2011 League Cup with Birmingham before moving to Sunderland on a free transfer as he was out of contract. He was sold to the Blues by Arsenal for £1m in 2007 after a successful loan deal. Larsson is regarded as one of the finest takers of set-pieces.

SHANE **LONG**

Position: Striker
Birth date: Jan 22, 1987
Birth place: Gortnahoe, Ireland
Height: 1.79m (5ft 11in)
Clubs: Cork City, Reading, West Brom
International: Republic of Ireland
Began senior career: 2004
It's a fact: Long was part of the £80,000 deal that took Kevin Doyle to Reading in 2005 – but was sold to West Brom for £4.5m in summer 2011. He had helped Reading to their first appearance in the Premier League in 2006 and was their Player of the Season when he left for the Hawthorns.

MAICON

Position: Defender
Birth date: July 26, 1981
Birth place: Novo Hamburgo, Brazil
Height: 1.84m (6ft 1in)
Clubs: Cruzeiro, Monaco, Inter Milan
International: Brazil
Began senior career: 2001
It's a fact: The raiding full back won the title in Brazil before moving to Europe. With Inter he has won four Serie A titles, two Italian Cups, three Italian Super Cups, a European Cup and a World Club Cup. He has twice won both the Copa America and Confederations Cup with Brazil.

JAMES McCLEAN

Position: Midfielder
Birth date: April 22, 1989
Birth place: Derry, Northern Ireland
Height: 1.8m (5ft 11in)
Clubs: Institute, Derry City, Sunderland
International: Republic of Ireland
Began senior career: 2007
It's a fact: McClean cost Sunderland just £350,000 in summer 2011. He had won the League of Ireland with Derry. The Black Cats' Young Player of the Season at the end of his first term. Plays for the Republic despite having turned out for Northern Ireland's Under-21 side.

JUAN MATA

Position: Midfielder
Birth date: April 28, 1988
Birth place: Ocon de Villafranca, Spain
Height: 1.7m (5ft 7in)
Clubs: Real Madrid, Valencia, Chelsea
International: Spain
Began senior career: 2006
It's a fact: Chelsea's £23.5m buy in summer 2011 had already won the Copa del Rey with Valencia. A World Cup-winner with Spain in 2010 he added Euro 2012 to the FA Cup and European Cup lifted during his first campaign as a Blues player.

JAMES MILNER

Position: Midfielder
Birth date: January 4, 1986
Birth place: Leeds
Height: 1.76m (5ft 9in)
Clubs: Leeds United, Swindon Town (loan), Newcastle United, Aston Villa, Manchester City
International: England
Began senior career: 2002
It's a fact: Milner played a record 30 times for England Under-21s. Once the youngest player to score in the Premier League – nine days before his 17th birthday. An FA Cup and Premier League winner with City.

LUKA MODRIC

Position: Midfielder
Birth date: Sept 9, 1985
Birth place: Zadar, Yugoslavia
Height: 1.73m (5ft 8in)
Clubs: Dinamo Zagreb, Zrinjski Mostar (loan), Inter Zapresic (loan), Tottenham
International: Croatia
Began senior career: 2003
It's a fact: Modric picked up three league winners' medals with Zagreb in 2006, 2007 and 2008. He also won the Croatian Cup and Super Cup. Spurs' Player of the Season in 2011 and Bosnia Player of the Year 2003.

THOMAS **MULLER**

Position: Midfielder
Birth date: September 13, 1989
Birth place: Weilheim, Germany
Height: 1.86m (6ft 1in)
Clubs: Bayern Munich
International: Germany
Began senior career: 2008
It's a fact: Muller was the Best Young Player at World Cup 2010 and also won the Golden Boot as the finals' top scorer with five goals. Has won one Bundesliga title, a German Cup and German Super Cup. An ever-present for Bayern from 2009-10 to 2011-12.

YOUSSOUF **MULUMBU**

Position: Midfielder
Birth date: January 25, 1987
Birth place: Kinshasa, DR Congo
Height: 1.77m (5ft 10in)
Clubs: Paris Saint Germain, Amiens (loan), West Brom
International: DR Congo
Began senior career: 2004
It's a fact: Mulumbu played for France up to Under-21 level, then agreed to make his senior debut for DR Congo, before announcing his international retirement in 2011 after collecting 12 caps. Voted West Brom's 2011-11 Player of the Year by both fans and players.

NANI

Position: Winger
Birth date: Nov 17, 1986
Birth place: Praia, Cape Verde
Height: 1.75m (5ft 9in)
Clubs: Sporting Lisbon, Manchester United
International: Portugal
Began senior career: 2005
It's a fact: He was voted Manchester United Player of the Season by his own team-mates in 2011 yet failed to get on the shortlist for the PFA award. Signed by United for £18m in 2007 and has since won three Premier League titles, a League Cup, European Cup and Club World Cup.

SAMIR **NASRI**

Position: Midfielder
Birth date: June 26, 1987
Birth place: Marseille, France
Height: 1.77m (5ft 10in)
Clubs: Marseille, Arsenal, Manchester City
International: France
Began senior career: 2004
It's a fact: Arsenal doubled their money when they sold Nasri. They bought him for around £12m in 2008 and sold him to Man City for £25m in summer 2011. Lique 1 Young Player of the Year in 2007 and French Player of the Year 2010, his first year with City brought him the Premier League title.

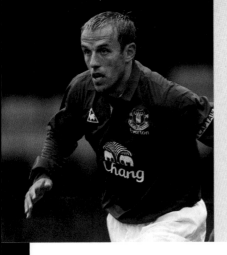

PHIL **NEVILLE**

Position: Midfielder
Birth date: Jan 21, 1977
Birth place: Bury, Manchester
Height: 1.8m (5ft 11in)
Clubs: Man United, Everton
International: England
Began senior career: 1995
It's a fact: The younger brother of former England right back Gary moved to Everton in 2005 – and made his Premier League debut for them against his brother! Won six Premier League titles, three FA Cups, a European Cup and Intercontinental Cup with United. Earned 59 England caps from 1996-07.

Everton

NEYMAR

Position: Striker
Birth date: February 5, 1992
Birth place: Sao Paulo, Brazil
Height: 1.74m (5ft 9in)
Clubs: Santos
International: Brazil
Began senior career: 2009
It's a fact: Neymar da Silva Santos Júnior has been the subject of interest and bids from many big European sides but said he wants to stay in his home country until after the 2014 World Cup is played there. The 2011 South American Footballer of the Year.

JI-SUNG **PARK**

Position: Midfielder
Birth date: February 25, 1981
Birth place: Seoul, South Korea
Height: 1.77m (5ft 10in)
Clubs: Kyoto Purple Sanga, PSV Eindhoven, Manchester United, QPR
International: South Korea
Began senior career: 2002
It's a fact: Park captained his country and won a total of 100 South Korea caps from 2000-2011. Won two Dutch titles and a Dutch Cup with PSV and moved to United for £4.5m in 2005. Has now added four Premier League titles, three League Cups, a Club World Cup and European Cup medal.

SCOTT **PARKER**

Position: Midfielder
Birth date: Oct 13, 1980
Birth place: Lambeth, South London
Height: 1.75m (5ft 9in)
Clubs: Charlton, Norwich (loan) Chelsea, Newcastle United, West Ham, Tottenham
International: England
Began senior career: 1997
It's a fact: FWA Footballer of the Year and England Player of the Year for 2011. Parker was also Charlton Player of the Year 2003 and Hammer of the Year 2009, 2010 and 2011.

TOTTENHAM HOTSPUR

ALEXANDRE **PATO**

Position: Striker
Birth date: September 2, 1989
Birth place: Parana, Brazil
Height: 1.79m (5ft 10in)
Clubs: Internacional, AC Milan
International: Brazil
Began senior career: 2006
It's a fact: Pato had been with Internacional for just one season before he was transferred to AC Milan in 2007 for £20m. He had already won a Club World Cup and South America Supercup. Pato added a Serie A title and Italian Super Cup to his honours in 2011.

PEDRO

Position: Winger
Birth date: July 28, 1987
Birth place: Santa Cruz de Tenerife, Spain
Height: 1.65m (5ft 5in)
Clubs: Barcelona
International: Spain
Began senior career: 2005
It's a fact: His full name is Pedro Eliezer Rodríguez Ledesma and he is one of the shortest players in La Liga. That's not stopped him picking up three La Liga titles, two Copa del Reys, three Spanish Super Cups, two European Cups, a UEFA Super Cup, Club World Cup, plus the 2010 World Cup and Euro 2012!

ROBIN **VAN PERSIE**

Position: Striker
Birth date: Aug 6, 1983
Birth place: Rotterdam, Holland
Height: 1.83m (6ft)
Clubs: Feyenoord, Arsenal
International: Holland
Began senior career: 2001
It's a fact: RVP's 35 goals in 2011 left him just one short of Alan Shearer's record haul for one year. A UEFA Cup winner at Feyenoord, he won the FA Cup at Arsenal and was a beaten European Cup finalist. PFA Players' and Fans' Player of the Year 2012, Arsenal Player of the Season 2009 and 2012.

AARON **RAMSEY**

Position: Midfielder
Birth date: December 26, 1990
Birth place: Caerphilly, Wales
Height: 1.81m (5ft 11in)
Clubs: Cardiff City, Arsenal, Nottingham Forest (loan), Cardiff City (loan)
International: Wales
Began senior career: 2006
It's a fact: Ramsey became the youngest-ever captain of his country when he wore the armband at the age of 20 years and 90 days against England in March 2011. Wales' Young Player of the Year 2009 and 2010. Bought by Arsenal for £5m in 2008.

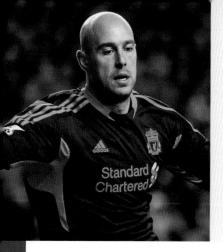

PEPE **REINA**

Position: Keeper
Birth date: Aug 31, 1982
Birth place: Madrid
Height: 1.88m (6ft 2in)
Clubs: Barcelona, Villarreal, Liverpool
International: Spain
Began senior career: 1999
It's a fact: Reina has won an FA Cup, League Cup and UEFA Super Cup since joining Liverpool in 2005. He was also been part of Spain's successful squad at Euro 2008 and 2012 and World Cup 2010.

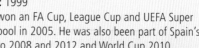

FRANCK **RIBERY**

Position: Winger
Birth date: April 7, 1983
Birth place: Boulogne-sur-Mer, France
Height: 1.7m (5ft 7in)
Clubs: Boulogne, Ales, Stade Brestois, Metz, Galatasaray, Marseille, Bayern Munich
International: France
Began senior career: 2000
It's a fact: He won Player of the Year awards in both France and Germany and helped Galatasaray win the Turkey Cup. Two Bundesliga titles, two German Cup and a German League Cup with Bayern.

MICAH **RICHARDS**

Position: Defender
Birth date: June 24, 1988
Birth place: Birmingham
Height: 1.8m (5ft 11in)
Clubs: Manchester City
International: England
Began senior career: 2005
It's a fact: When he played for England against Holland at the age of 18 in 2006 he was the youngest-ever defender to turn out for the Three Lions. An FA Cup winner in 2011 and Premier League champion in 2012 he has played over 200 games for City. Selected for Team GB at the 2012 Olympics.

ARJEN **ROBBEN**

Position: Winger
Birth date: January 23, 1984
Birth place: Bedum, Holland
Height: 1.83m (6ft)
Clubs: Groningen, PSV Eindhoven, Chelsea, Real Madrid, Bayern Munich
International: Holland
Began senior career: 2000
It's a fact: Won the Eredivisie with PSV and joined Chelsea in 2004 for £12m. Moved to Real Madrid for £25m in 2007 having won two Premier Leagues, an FA Cup and two League Cups. One La Liga and a Spanish Super Cup at Madrid. A Bundesliga, a German Cup and German Super Cup at Bayern.

JACK **RODWELL**

Everton

Position: Midfielder
Birth date: March 11, 1991
Birth place: Southport, Lancashire
Height: 1.88m (6ft 2in)
Clubs: Everton
International: England
Began senior career: 2007
It's a fact: Rodwell played for Everton's reserves at the age of 15 and became their youngest-ever player in Europe at the age of 16 years and 284 days. Has represented England at all levels from Under-16 to senior level, making his full debut in a friendly against Spain in November 2011.

CRISTIANO **RONALDO**

Position: Midfielder
Birth date: February 5, 1985
Birth place: Funchal, Madeira
Height: 1.86m (6ft 1in)
Clubs: Sporting Lisbon, Manchester United, Real Madrid
International: Portugal
Began senior career: 2002
It's a fact: His £80m move from United to Madrid in summer 2009 set a new world record transfer fee. Three Premier Leagues, an FA Cup, two League Cups, a European Cup and Club World Cup with United. He has won one La Liga and the Copa del Rey with Madrid.

WAYNE **ROONEY**

Position: Striker
Birth date: Oct 24, 1985
Birth place: Croxteth, Liverpool
Height: 1.76m (5ft 9in)
Clubs: Everton, Man United
International: England
Began senior career: 2002
It's a fact: When Rooney moved from Everton to United in 2004 the initial £25.6m transfer fee set a new record for a player under the age of 20. It later rose to £30m. Four Premier League titles, two League Cups, a European Cup and Club World Cup with United. Three-times Goal of the Season winner.

JOHN **RUDDY**

Position: Keeper
Birth date: October 24, 1986
Birth place: St. Ives, Cambridgeshire
Height: 1.93m (6ft 4in)
Clubs: Cambridge United, Everton, Walsall (loan), Rushden (loan), Chester City (loan), Wrexham (loan), Bristol City (loan), Stockport County (loan), Crewe Alexandra (loan), Norwich City
International: England
Began senior career: 2004
It's a fact: Ruddy joined Norwich in 2010 and helped them reach the Premier League. Called into England's Euro 2012 squad but was then injured.

BACARY **SAGNA**

Position: Defender
Birth date: February 14, 1983
Birth place: Bourgogne, France
Height: 1.76m (5ft 9in)
Clubs: Auxerre, Arsenal
International: France
Began senior career: 2002
It's a fact: Won the French Cup at Auxerre and was their 2007 Player of the Season. Then joined Arsenal for 2007-08 where the full back was named in the PFA Team of the Year after his first full season with the Gunners. Voted into Premier League Team of the Year for 2007-08 and 2010-11.

CHRISTOPHER **SAMBA**

Position: Defender
Birth date: March 28, 1984
Birth place: Creteil, France
Height: 1.93m (6ft 4in)
Clubs: Sedan, Hertha Berlin, Blackburn Rovers, Anzhi Makhachkala
International: DR Congo
Began senior career: 2002
It's a fact: The giant centre half cost Rovers just £450,000 in 2007 and was sold to Anzhi in February 2012 for £12.5m. Played 184 games in almost six seasons with the Ewood Park side. Won 26 DR Congo caps between 2004-08 and has said he hopes to play for them once again.

ALEXIS **SANCHEZ**

Position: Striker
Birth date: December 19, 1988
Birth place: Tocopilla, Chile
Height: 1.69m (5ft 7in)
Clubs: Corbreloa, Udinese, Colo-Colo(loan), River Plate (loan), Barcelona
International: Chile
Began senior career: 2005
It's a fact: The first Chilean to play for Barcelona cost £23m in 2011 – and that fee could rise by £10m. Won two Chilean titles and a Copa Sudamericana with Colo-Colo, plus one Argentina title with River Plate. A Copa del Rey, Spanish Super Cup, UEFA Super Cup and Club World Cup at Barcelona.

SANDRO

Position: Midfielder
Birth date: March 15, 1989
Birth place: Minas Gerais, Brazil
Height: 1.87m (6ft 2in)
Clubs: Internacional, Tottenham
International: Brazil
Began senior career: 2008
It's a fact: Sandro signed for Tottenham in 2010 following an £8m transfer and a year later extended his contract to 2016. At Internacional he had won two titles, a Copa Sudamericana and Copa Libertadores. Made his senior debut for Brazil in 2009.

BASTIAN **SCHWEINSTEIGER**

Position: Midfielder
Birth date: August 1, 1984
Birth place: Kolbermoor, Germany
Height: 1.83m (6ft)
Clubs: Bayern Munich
International: Germany
Began senior career: 2002
It's a fact: Having made his international debut in 2004, he was called up for that year's Euros and also played at Euro 2008 and 2012. Played in the World Cup finals of 2006 and 2010. Has won five Bundesligas, five German Cups, two German League Cups and a German Super Cup with Bayern.

STEPHANE **SESSEGNON**

Position: Midfielder
Birth date: June 1, 1984
Birth place: Allahe, Benin
Height: 1.7m (5ft 7in)
Clubs: Requins de l'Atlantique, Creteil, Le Mans, Paris Saint Germain, Sunderland
International: Benin
Began senior career: 2003
It's a fact: Sessegnon, who cost Sunderland £6m from PSG in January 2011, was the first Benin player in the Premier League. He was the Black Cats' Player of the Year in 2012. Won the French Cup with Paris Saint Germain.

DAVID **SILVA**

Position: Midfielder
Birth date: Jan 8, 1986
Birth place: Arguineguin, Spain
Height: 1.7m (5ft 7in)
Clubs: Valencia, Eibar (loan), Celta Vigo (loan), Manchester City
International: Spain
Began senior career: 2003
It's a fact: City bought Silva from Valencia in summer 2010 for £24m. He had already won a Copa del Rey. Silva added an FA Cup and Premier League in his first two seasons in Manchester. A European Championships winner with Spain in 2008 and 2012 and World Cup victor in 2010.

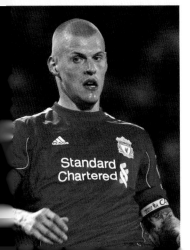

MARTIN **SKRTEL**

Position: Defender
Birth date: Dec 15, 1984
Birth place: Handlova, Czechoslovakia
Height: 1.91m (6ft 3in)
Clubs: Trencin, Zenit Saint Petersburg, Liverpool
International: Slovakia
Began senior career: 2001
It's a fact: Skrtel signed for Liverpool in January 2008 and took part in Slovakia's first-ever World Cup finals appearance in 2010. Won the Russian Premier League with Zenit and a League Cup with Liverpool. Slovak Footballer of the Year 2007, 2008 and 2011. Liverpool Player of the Season 2012.

CHRIS **SMALLING**

Position: Defender
Birth date: November 22, 1989
Birth place: Greenwich, London
Height: 1.92m (6ft 4in)
Clubs: Fulham, Manchester United
International: England
Began senior career: 2008
It's a fact: United paid Fulham £10m for Smalling in 2010 after he had played just four Premier League games. He has now won a Premier League title, two Community Shields and made his full England debut. Began his international career with England Schoolboys' Under-18 side.

WESLEY **SNEIJDER**

Position: Midfielder
Birth date: June 9, 1984
Birth place: Utrecht, Holland
Height: 1.7m (5ft 7in)
Clubs: Ajax, Real Madrid, Inter Milan
International: Holland
Began senior career: 2002
It's a fact: In the eleven games he played at Euro 2008 and World Cup 2010, Sneijder won six Man of the Match awards! Lifted an Eredivisie and Dutch Cup with Ajax; La Liga at Madrid; Serie A, two Italian Cups, an Italian Super Cup, a European Cup and Club World Cup at Inter.

ALEX **SONG**

Position: Defender
Birth date: September 9, 1987
Birth place: Douala, Cameroon
Height: 1.84m (6ft)
Clubs: Bastia, Arsenal, Charlton (loan)
International: Cameroon
Began senior career: 2004
It's a fact: Although he played for France at youth level, Song moved to the Cameroon Under-17 side and then committed to the country of his birth. Joined Arsenal for just £1m in 2006 and has now played more than 200 games for the Gunners.

DANIEL **STURRIDGE**

Position: Striker
Birth date: September 1, 1989
Birth place: Birmingham
Height: 1.88m (6ft 2in)
Clubs: Manchester City, Chelsea, Bolton (loan)
International: England
Began senior career: 2006
It's a fact: The striker could cost Chelsea £6m depending on his progress. The Blues also have to give 15 per cent of any transfer fee they receive to Manchester City. Since joining Chelsea in 2009 he has won a Premier League, two FA Cups, a European Cup and made his England debut.

LUIS **SUAREZ**

Position: Striker
Birth date: January 24, 1987
Birth place: Salto, Uruguay
Height: 1.81m (5ft 11in)
Clubs: Nacional, Groningen, Ajax, Liverpool
International: Uruguay
Began senior career: 2005
It's a fact: The former Dutch Footballer of the Year cost Liverpool £22.8m when he moved to Anfield in January 2011. Won the league title in Uruguay with Nacional; the Dutch title and Dutch Cup with Ajax; and League Cup at Liverpool. A Copa America victor with his country.

WOJCIECH **SZCZESNY**

Position: Keeper
Birth date: April 18, 1990
Birth place: Warsaw, Poland
Height: 1.95m (6ft 5in)
Clubs: Leiga Warsaw, Arsenal, Brentford (loan)
International: Poland
Began senior career: 2009
It's a fact: Szczesny moved to Arsenal from Legia Warsaw in 2006 as a youth player and has jumped ahead of three keepers who were above him for the No.1 jersey. Now his country's first-choice keeper – just like his father Maciej who won seven caps between 1991-96.

STEVEN **TAYLOR**

Position: Defender
Birth date: January 23, 1986
Birth place: Greenwich, London
Height: 1.88m (6ft 2in)
Clubs: Newcastle United, Wycombe (loan)
International: England
Began senior career: 2003
It's a fact: The former England Under-21 captain won 29 caps at that level having progressed from the Under-16s. He was part of Newcastle's Championship-winning side. When he came on against Mallorca in 2004 he was then the Magpies youngest player in Europe.

JOHN **TERRY**

Position: Defender
Birth date: December 7, 1980
Birth place: Barking, Essex
Height: 1.87m (6ft 1in)
Clubs: Chelsea, Nottingham Forest (loan)
International: England
Began senior career: 1998
It's a fact: JT was the first senior England player to score at the new Wembley and the first captain to lift the FA Cup under the arch. Has won three Premier Leagues with Chelsea, five FA Cups, two League Cups and a European Cup. Chelsea Player of the Year 2001 and 2006.

CHEICK **TIOTE**

Position: Midfielder
Birth date: June 21, 1986
Birth place: Yamoussoukro, Ivory Coast
Height: 1.77m (5ft 10in)
Clubs: Anderlecht, Roda (loan), Twente, Newcastle United
International: Ivory Coast
Began senior career: 2005
It's a fact: Tiote won two Belgian titles and two Belgian Super Cups with Anderlecht. He lifted the Eredivisie and Dutch Super Cup with Twente, where former England boss Steve McClaren was his gaffer. Joined Newcastle in summer 2010 for just £3.5m.

FERNANDO **TORRES**

Position: Striker
Birth date: March 20, 1984
Birth place: Fuenlabrada, Spain
Height: 1.83m (6ft)
Clubs: Atletico Madrid, Liverpool, Chelsea
International: Spain
Began senior career: 2001
It's a fact: Chelsea's £50m striker was the fastest player to reach 50 goals for Liverpool. It took him just 72 games. Has won the FA Cup and European Cup with the Blues. Part of Spain's winning sides at Euro 2008 and 2012 and World Cup 2010. The only player to score in two Euro finals.

KOLO **TOURE**

Position: Defender
Birth date: March 19, 1981
Birth place: Bouake, Ivory Coast
Height: 1.83m (6ft)
Clubs: ASEC Mimosas, Arsenal, Manchester City
International: Ivory Coast
Began senior career: 2002
It's a fact: Toure made more than 300 appearances for Arsenal during seven years at the club before moving to City in 2009 for £16m. Two Ivory Coast titles and an Ivorian Cup with ASEX; a Premier League and two FA Cups with Arsenal; an FA Cup and Premier League with Manchester City.

YAYA **TOURE**

Position: Midfielder
Birth date: May 13, 1983
Birth place: Bouake, Ivory Coast
Height: 1.92m (6ft 3in)
Clubs: Beveren, Metalurh, Olympiacos, Monaco, Barcelona, Manchester City
International: Ivory Coast
Began senior career: 2001
It's a fact: Kolo's younger brother won the Greek League and Greek Cup with Olympiacos. Won La Liga twice, a Copa del Rey, a Spanish Super Cup, a European Cup, UEFA Super Cup and Club World Cup at Barca. Joined City for £24m in 2010 and has won an FA Cup and Premier League.

THOMAS **VERMAELEN**

Position: Defender
Birth date: November 14, 1985
Birth place: Kapellen, Belgium
Height: 1.82m (6ft)
Clubs: Ajax, Waalwijk (loan), Arsenal
International: Belgium
Began senior career: 2003
It's a fact: Vermaelen scored on his debut for Arsenal, netting in the 6-1 victory at Everton in August 2009 following an £8m move from Ajax. Won the Eredivisie and two Dutch Cups during his six years at the Amsterdam Arena. Named in Premier League team of 2009-10.

RAFAEL **VAN DER VAART**

Position: Midfielder
Birth date: February 11, 1983
Birth place: Heemskerk, Holland
Height: 1.77m (5ft 9in)
Clubs: Ajax, Hamburg, Real Madrid, Tottenham
International: Holland
Began senior career: 2000
It's a fact: The Dutch maestro was Tottenham's top scorer with 13 goal in 2010-11, his first season in the Premier League following an £8m move from Madrid. Won two Eredivisie titles and a Dutch Cup at Ajax and the Spanish Super Cup with Madrid.

NEMANJA **VIDIC**

Position: Defender
Birth date: Oct 21, 1981
Birth place: Titovo Uzice, Yugoslavia
Height: 1.89m (6ft 2in)
Clubs: Red Star Belgrade, Spartak Subotica (loan), Spartak Moscow, Manchester United
International: Serbia
Began senior career: 2000
It's a fact: Barclays Player of the season 2009 and 2011. Won the title and Yugoslav Cup with Red Star. Four titles, three League Cups, a European Cup and Club World Cup with United. Twice Serbia Footballer of the Year.

DAVID **VILLA**

Position: Striker
Birth date: December 3, 1981
Birth place: Langreo, Spain
Height: 1.75m (5ft 9in)
Clubs: Sporting Gijon, Zaragoza, Valencia, Barcelona
International: Spain
Began senior career: 1999
It's a fact: Spain's record scorer has also lifted the 2010 World Cup and Euro 2008. Won Copa del Rey and Spanish Super Cup with Zaragoza; Copa del Rey at Valencia; one La Liga, a European Cup, Copa del Rey, Spanish Super Cup, UEFA Super Cup and Club World Cup at Barca.

THEO **WALCOTT**

Position: Striker
Birth date: March 16, 1989
Birth place: Stanmore, West London
Height: 1.75m (5ft 9in)
Clubs: Southampton, Arsenal
International: England
Began senior career: 2004
It's a fact: Walcott was just 16 when he joined Arsenal for an initial £5m in January 2006, a fee that would rise to £12m. Selected for England's 2006 World Cup squad but did not play in Germany. Hit a hat-trick against Croatia in a World Cup 2010 qualifier.

KYLE **WALKER**

Position: Defender
Birth date: May 28, 1990
Birth place: Sheffield
Height: 1.78m (5ft 10in)
Clubs: Sheffield United, Northampton (loan), Tottenham, Sheffield United (loan), QPR (loan), Aston Villa (loan)
International: England
Began senior career: 2008
It's a fact: Walker joined Spurs in 2009 but was loaned back to Sheffield United, his boyhood heroes, for the following season. PFA Young Player of the Year 2012, made his full England debut against Spain in November 2011.

STEPHEN **WARNOCK**

Position: Defender
Birth date: December 12, 1981
Birth place: Ormskirk, Lancashire
Height: 1.78m (5ft 10in)
Clubs: Liverpool, Bradford City (loan), Coventry City (loan), Blackburn Rovers, Aston Villa
International: England
Began senior career: 2002
It's a fact: Sold by Liverpool to Blackburn for £2.5 in 2007, he moved to Villa for £8m in 2009. Won the European Cup at Liverpool, along with an FA Cup and UEFA Super Cup. Blackburn's 2009 Player of the Season.

DANNY **WELBECK**

Position: Striker
Birth date: November 26, 1990
Birth place: Manchester
Height: 1.85m (6ft 1in)
Clubs: Manchester United, Preston (loan), Sunderland (loan)
International: England
Began senior career: 2008
It's a fact: The forward could have played for Ghana but decided to play international football for England – and made his senior debut against Ghana at Wembley in 2011. A League Cup and Club World Cup winner with United.

ASHLEY **WILLIAMS**

Position: Defender
Birth date: August 23, 1984
Birth place: Tamworth, Staffordshire
Height: 1.83m (6ft)
Clubs: Stockport County, Swansea City
International: Wales
Began senior career: 2003
It's a fact: Released by West Brom as a youngster, Williams had just three League One games on loan with Swansea before they signed him for around £500,000 in 2008. Part of the Swans side that won promotion to the Premier League via the play-offs in 2010-11.

JACK **WILSHERE**

Position: Midfielder
Birth date: January 1, 1992
Birth place: Stevenage, Hertfordshire
Height: 1.73m (5ft 8in)
Clubs: Arsenal, Bolton (loan)
International: England
Began senior career: 2008
It's a fact: He joined Arsenal at the age of nine and was their youngest-ever League player in 2008 at the age of 16 years and 256 days. An FA Youth Cup winner in 2009, in 2011 he was Arsenal's Player of the Season and the PFA Young Player of the Year. Voted into PFA Team of the Year 2011.

XAVI

Position: Midfielder
Birth date: January 25, 1980
Birth place: Terrassa, Spain
Height: 1.7m (5ft 7in)
Clubs: Barcelona
International: Spain
Began senior career: 1997
It's a fact: He's made more than 115 appearances for Spain and around 700 for Barcelona! Won Euro 2008 and 2012 and the 2010 World Cup with Spain. Six La Ligas with Barca, plus two Copa del Rey, five Spanish Super Cups, three European Cups, two UEFA Super Cups and two Club World Cups.

ASHLEY **YOUNG**

Position: Winger
Birth date: July 9, 1985
Birth place: Stevenage, Hertfordshire
Height: 1.75m (5ft 9in)
Clubs: Watford, Aston Villa, Manchester United
International: England
Began senior career: 2003
It's a fact: Watford received a club record £9.75m Aston Villa when Young left Vicarage Road in 2007. He moved to United for £15m in 2011. Watford Player of the Season 2005; Championship Team of the Year 2006; Premier League Team of the Year 2008, 2009, PFA Young Player of the Year 2009.

LEGENDS

W here do you start and where do you finish when you list legends of football? The answer is that no list is definitive. We all have our ideas on who has made a massive impact on the beautiful game. But the players listed here are ones that you should certainly be aware of!

TONY **ADAMS**

Position: Defender
Birth date: October 10, 1966
Birth place: Romford, Essex
Height: 1.91m (6ft 3in)
Club: Arsenal
International: England (66 caps, 5 goals)
Pro career: 1983-02
It's a fact: Between 1983 and 2002, Adams turned out in 672 games for the Gunners having been appointed their captain at the age of 21. He won four titles, three FA Cups, two League Cups and a UEFA Cup Winners' Cup and was PFA Young Player of the Year in 1987.

ROBERTO **BAGGIO**

Position: Striker
Birth date: February 18, 1967
Birth place: Caldogno, Italy
Height: 1.74m (5ft 9in)
Clubs: Vicenza, Fiorentina, Juventus, AC Milan, Bologna, Inter Milan, Brescia
International: Italy (56 caps, 27 goals)
Pro career: 1982-04
It's a fact: Baggio, 1993 World Player of the Year and Ballon D'Or winner, also scored at three World Cup finals. He won Serie A during his time with AC Milan; the tile and UEFA Cup with Juventus; and the InterToto Cup with Bologna. Noted for his ponytail hairstyle and his amazing ball skills.

GORDON **BANKS**

Position: Keeper
Birth date: December 30, 1937
Birth place: Sheffield
Height: 1.85m (6ft 1in)
Clubs: Chesterfield, Leicester City, Stoke City, Cleveland Stoker (loan), Hellenic (loan), Fort Lauderdale Strikers (loan), St. Patrick's Athletic (loan).
International: England (73 caps, 0 goals)
Pro career: 1955-77
It's a fact: Banks is credited with pulling off the greatest-ever save in a World Cup finals game when he stopped a header from Pele. A World Cup-winner with England, Banks lifted the League Cup with Leicester and Stoke.

MARCO **VAN BASTEN**

Position: Striker
Birth date: October 31, 1964
Birth place: Utrecht, Holland
Height: 1.88m (6ft 2in)
Clubs: Ajax, AC Milan
International: Holland (58 caps, 24 goals)
Pro career: 1982-95
It's a fact: Van Basten scored 278 goals in 376 club games before his career was cut short by injury. European Footballer of the Year in 1988, 1989 and 1992 he was also World Player of the Year in 1992. Won three European Cups and Serie A four times with Milan and three Dutch League titles with Ajax.

FRANZ **BECKENBAUER**

Position: Defender
Birth date: September 11, 1945
Birth place: Munich
Height: 1.81m (5ft 11in)
Clubs: Bayern Munich, New York Cosmos, Hamburg
International: Germany (103 caps, 14 goals)
Pro career: 1964-83
It's a fact: Der Kaiser, or The Emperor, has won the German Bundesliga both as a manager and player – and also lifted the World Cup as both boss and player! Five times a Bundesliga winner as a player, five times with Bayern and once at Hamburg, he has lifted the trophy once, as boss of Bayern.

DENNIS **BERGKAMP**

Position: Forward
Birth date: May 10, 1969
Birth place: Amsterdam
Height: 1.88m (6ft 2in)
Clubs: Ajax, Inter Milan, Arsenal
International: Holland (79 caps, 37 goals)
Pro career: 1986-2006
It's a fact: His last appearance as a player was in the 2006 Champions League Final when Arsenal lost 2-1 to Barcelona. Bergkamp won three Premier League titles and four FA Cups with the Gunners. An Eredivisie winner with Ajax, plus four Dutch Cups, a UEFA Cup and a Cup Winners' Cup.

GEORGE **BEST**

Position: Midfielder
Birth date: May 22, 1946
Birth place: Belfast, Northern Ireland
Height: 1.75m (5ft 9in)
Clubs: Manchester United, Los Angeles Aztecs, Fulham, Fort Lauderdale Strikers, Hibs, San Jose Earthquakes, Bournemouth
International: Northern Ireland (37 games, 9 goals).
Pro career: 1963-83
It's a fact: Best, often regarded as the first celebrity footballer, tragically died in 2005 at the age of 59. He was one of the first players in the English Football Hall of Fame. Won two league titles and a European Cup with United.

BILLY **BREMNER**

Position: Midfielder
Birth date: December 9, 1942
Birth place: Stirling, Scotland
Height: 1.66m (5ft 5in)
Clubs: Leeds United, Hull City, Doncaster Rovers
International: Scotland (54 caps, 3 goals)
Pro career: 1959-81
It's a fact: Bremner, voted Leeds' greatest player of all time, died in 1997 at the aged of 54. Among his honours were two league titles and an FA Cup with Leeds. One of the traditional hard-men midfielders his legend lives on thanks to a statue outside of Elland Road.

GIANLUIGI **BUFFON**

Position: Keeper
Birth date: January 28, 1978
Birth place: Carrara, Italy
Height: 1.91m (6ft 3in)
Clubs: Parma, Juventus
International: Italy (118 caps, 0 goals)
Pro career: 1995-present
It's a fact: Buffon is the world's most expensive goalkeeper and cost Juventus £32.6m in 2001. He has been Serie A keeper of the year eight times. Three-times a Serie A winner, he has also won the UEFA Cup, Italian Cup, Italian Super Cup (3) and was a World Cup winner in 2006.

TERRY **BUTCHER**

Position: Defender
Birth date: December 28, 1958
Birth place: Singapore
Height: 1.93m (6ft 4in)
Clubs: Ipswich, Rangers, Coventry, Sunderland, Clydebank
International: England (77 caps, 3 goals)
Pro career: 1976-93
It's a fact: The central defender won the UEFA Cup with Ipswich plus three Scottish titles and two Scottish Cups with Rangers. A tough but skilled player he moved into management after retiring. Ironically for a player so highly regarded in an England shirt he is in the Scottish Football Hall of Fame!

FABIO **CANNAVARO**

Position: Defender
Birth date: September 13, 1973
Birth place: Naples, Italy
Height: 1.76m (5ft 9in)
Clubs: Napoli, Parma, Inter Milan, Juventus, Real Madrid, Juventus, Al-Ahli
International: Italy (136 games, 2 goals)
Pro career: 1992-11
It's a fact: When he retired from international duty in 2010 Cannavaro's games made him Italy's record appearance holder. He won two La Liga titles with Real Madrid along with the Spanish Supercup plus two Italian Cups, the Italian Super Cup and UEFA Cup at Parma. A 2006 World Cup-winner.

ERIC **CANTONA**

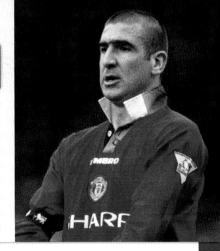

Position: Forward
Birth date: May 24, 1966
Birth place: Marseille, France
Height: 1.88m (6ft 2in)
Clubs: Auxerre, Martigues (loan), Marseille, Bordeaux (loan), Montpellier (loan), Nimes, Leeds United, Manchester United
International: France (45 caps, 20 goals)
Pro career: 1983-97
It's a fact: Cantona switched from Leeds to Man United for just £1.2m in 1992 and helped the Red Devils win four Premier Leagues and two FA Cups. Infamously banned eight months for kung-fu kicking a Crystal Palace fan.

BOBBY **CHARLTON**

Position: Forward
Birth date: October 11, 1937
Birth place: Ashington, Northumberland
Height: 1.73m (5ft 8in)
Clubs: Manchester United, Preston North End, Waterford
International: England (106 goals, 49 games)
Pro career: 1956-76
It's a fact: is United's former record appearance holder with 758 games and was a member of England's 1966 World Cup-winning side. Lifted three league titles, an FA Cup and European Cup with the Red Devils. United's record goalscorer with 249 and England's best with 49.

JACK **CHARLTON**

Position: Central defender
Birth date: May 8, 1935
Birth place: Ashington, Northumberland
Height: 1.91m (6ft 3in)
Clubs: Leeds United
International: England (35 games 6 goals)
Pro career: 1952-73
It's a fact: Old brother of Bobby, Jack was also part of England's 1966 World Cup side. He played 629 times for Leeds and scored 70 goals. Later managed Middlesbrough, Sheffield Wednesday, Newcastle United and had ten years in charge of the Republic of Ireland side.

BRIAN **CLOUGH**

Position: Striker
Birth date: March 21, 1935
Birth place: Middlesbrough
Height: 1.78m (5ft 10in)
Clubs: Middlesbrough, Sunderland
International: England (2 games, 0 goals)
Pro career: 1955-64
It's a fact: Clough scored an amazing 251 goals in 274 League games before injury ended his career at the age of 29. Later made his name by lifting the league title at both Nottingham Forest and Derby. Also won back-to-back European Cups with Forest in 1979 and 1980. He died in 2004.

JOHAN **CRUYFF**

Position: Forward
Birth date: April 25, 1947
Birth place: Amsterdam
Height: 1.8m (5ft 11in)
Clubs: Ajax, Barcelona, LA Aztecs, Washington Diplomats, Levante, Ajax, Feyenoord
International: Holland
Pro career: 1964-84
It's a fact: The Dutchman was a three times European Footballer of the Year and lifted the same title in Holland on four occasions. Eight times an Eredivisie winner with Ajax, once with Feyenoord. Won a Lag Liga at Barca.

KENNY **DALGLISH**

Position: Forward
Birth date: March 4, 1951
Birth place: Glasgow
Height: 1.73m (5ft 8in)
Clubs: Celtic, Liverpool
International: Scotland (102 caps, 30 goals)
Pro career: 1969-90
It's a fact: Dalglish won the English top-flight title eight times with Liverpool. Five of the titles were as a player, once as player-manger and twice as just manager. He won the Premier League title as manager of Blackburn Rovers. One of Liverpool's greatest players, he is Scotland's record appearance maker.

DIXIE **DEAN**

Position: Striker
Birth date: January 22, 1907
Birth place: Birkenhead, Wirrall
Height: 1.78m (5ft 10in)
Clubs: Tranmere, Everton, Notts County, Sligo Rovers, Hurst
International: England (16 caps, 18 goals)
Pro career: 1923-40
It's a fact: Dean died at the age of 73 but is immortalised in a statue outside Everton's Goodison Park. He scored 60 league goals for the club in 1927-28, still an English best. Also hit an astounding 37 hat-tricks for the Toffees as he lifted two league titles and an FA Cup during his time with the club.

PAOLO **DI CANIO**

Position: Striker
Birth date: July 9, 1968
Birth place: Rome
Height: 1.78m (5ft 10in)
Clubs: Lazio, Terana (loan), Juventus, Napoli, AC Milan, Celtic, Sheffield Wednesday, West Ham, Charlton, Lazio, Cisco Roma
International: Italy Under-21 (9 caps, 2 goals)
Pro career: 1985-08
It's a fact: Banned for 11 Wednesday games in 1998 after pushing referee Paul Alcock, Di Canio won a Fair Play Award three years later when he kicked the ball out rather than score so the Everton keeper could get treatment.

ALFREDO **DI STEFANO**

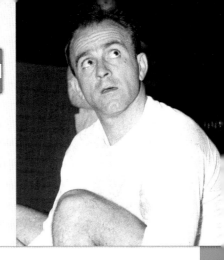

Position: Forward
Birth date: July 4, 1926
Birth place: Buenos Aires, Argentina
Height: 1.78m (5ft 10in)
Clubs: River Plate, Huracan (loan), Millonarios, Real Madrid, Espanyol
International: Argentina (6 caps, 6 goals), Colombia (4 caps, 0 goals), Spain (31 caps, 23 goals)
Pro career: 1945-66
It's a fact: The 1957 and 1959 European Footballer of the Year won eight La Liga titles and five European Cups during his time with Madrid. Real's second highest scorer of all-time with 216 goals in 282 league games.

EUSEBIO

Position: Forward
Birth date: January 25, 1942
Birth place: Lourenco Marques, East Africa
Height: 1.75m (5ft 9in)
Clubs: Sporting de Lourenco Marques, Benfica, Boston Minutemen, Monterrey, Toronto Metros, Beira-Mar, Las Vegas Quicksilvers, Uniao de Tomar, New Jersey Americans
International: Portugal (64 caps, 41 goals)
Pro career: 1957-79
It's a fact: Eusebio won 11 Portuguese titles with Benfica where he played 614 games and scored a club record 638 goals. He also won five Portuguese Cups and a European Cup.

LUIS **FIGO**

Position: Midfielder
Birth date: November 4, 1972
Birth place: Lisbon, Portugal
Height: 1.8m (5ft 11in)
Clubs: Sporting, Barcelona, Real Madrid, Inter Milan
International: Portugal (127 caps, 32 goals)
Pro career: 1989-09
It's a fact: Portugal's most-capped player with 127 appearances, Figo was European Player of the Year in 2000 and World Player of the Year 2001. Transferred from Barcelona where he had won two La Ligas to Madrid for £37m in 2000 and won two more titles. Added four Serie A titles at Inter.

PAUL **GASCOIGNE**

Position: Midfielder
Birth date: May 27, 1967
Birth place: Gateshead
Height: 1.75m (5ft 9in)
Clubs: Newcastle, Tottenham, Lazio, Rangers, Middlesbrough, Everton, Burnley, Gansu Tianma
International: England (57 caps, 10 goals)
Pro career: 1985-04
It's a fact: When Gazza moved from Newcastle to Tottenham in 1988 the £2m fee was a then British record. Four years later he moved to Lazio for £5.5m. Famed for his tears when he was booked in the semi-final of Italia 90.

JIMMY **GREAVES**

Position: Striker
Birth date: February 20, 1940
Birth place: Manor Park, East London
Height: 1.73m (5ft 8in)
Clubs: Chelsea, AC Milan, Tottenham, West Ham, Brentwood, Chelmsford City, Barnet
International: England (57 caps, 44 goals)
Pro career: 1957-79
It's a fact: Greavsie scored a club record 266 goals in 379 games for Tottenham. He created a record of being the league's top scorer for six seasons during his time with Spurs and Chelsea.

RUUD **GULLIT**

Position: Midfielder
Birth date: September 1, 1962
Birth place: Amsterdam
Height: 1.86m (6ft 1in)
Clubs: Haarlem, Feyenoord, PSV Eindhoven, AC Milan, Samdoria, AC Milan, Sampdoria (loan), Chelsea
International: Holland (66 caps, 17 goals)
Pro career: 1979-98
It's a fact: Gullit captained Holland to success at Euro 88, the year after becoming European Footballer of the Year. He was an FA Cup winner with Chelsea in 1997.

THIERRY **HENRY**

Position: Striker
Birth date: August 17, 1977
Birth place: Paris
Height: 1.88m (6ft 2in)
Clubs: Monaco, Juventus, Arsenal, Barcelona, New York Red Bulls, Arsenal (loan)
International: France (123 caps, 51 goals)
Pro career: 1994-present
It's a fact: Henry is Arsenal's all-time record goal scorer with 228 goals in 376 games, has twice been PFA Player of the Year and lifted the Football Writers' Footballer of the Year award three times.

GLENN **HODDLE**

Position: Midfielder
Birth date: October 27, 1957
Birth place: Hayes, West London
Height: 1.83m (6ft)
Clubs: Tottenham, Monaco, Swindon Town, Chelsea
International: England (53 caps, 8 goals)
Pro career: 1975-95
It's a fact: Hoddle, one of England's finest footballing talents, won two FA Cups and a League Cup with Spurs. A League and Cup winner at Monaco, he also won the FA Cup with Chelsea. Player manager of Swindon and Chelsea before taking the England job. Also boss of Southampton, Spurs and Wolves.

GEOFF **HURST**

Position: Striker
Birth date: December 8, 1941
Birth place: Ashton-under-Lyne, Cheshire
Height: 1.82m (5ft 11in)
Clubs: West Ham, Stoke City, Cape Town City (loan), West Brom, Cork Celtic, Seattle Sounders, Kuwait SC,
International: England (49 caps, 24 goals)
Pro career: 1959-76
It's a fact: Hurst is still the only player to have scored a hat-trick in a World Cup Final – as England beat Germany 4-2 at Wembley in 1966. He was knighted in 1998. Won the Cup Winners' Cup and FA Cup with West Ham.

ROY **KEANE**

Position: Midfielder
Birth date: August 10, 1971
Birth place: Cork, Eire
Height: 1.78m (5ft 10in)
Clubs: Nottingham Forest, Manchester United, Celtic
International: Republic of Ireland (67 caps, 9 goals)
Pro career: 1989-06
It's a fact: The United and Republic captain picked up seven Premier League titles, four FA Cups and a European Cup during his time at Old Trafford. The PFA Player of the Year and Football Writers' Footballer of the Year in 2000, he also won the Scottish Premier League and Scottish Cup with Celtic in 2006.

KEVIN **KEEGAN**

Position: Striker
Birth date: February 14, 1951
Birth place: Doncaster, South Yorkshire
Height: 1.73m (5ft 8in)
Clubs: Scunthorpe, Liverpool, Hamburg, Southampton, Newcastle United
International: England (63 caps, 21 goals)
Pro career: 1968-84
It's a fact: Keegan won the Ballon d'Or as European Football of the Year in 1978 and 1979 during his time at Hamburg. He won the Football Writers' award in 1976 and PFA accolade in 1982. He was also a European Cup winner with Liverpool in 1977.

JURGEN **KLINSMANN**

Position: Striker
Birth date: July 30, 1964
Birth place: Goppingen, Germany
Height: 1.81m (5ft 11in)
Clubs: Stuttgarter Kickers, Stuttgart, Inter Milan, Monaco, Tottenham, Bayern Munich, Sampdoria, Tottenham (loan)
International: Germany (108 caps, 47 goals)
Pro career: 1981-98
It's a fact: A World Cup 1990 and Euro 96 winner with Germany, Klinsmann was 1995 Football Writers' Footballer of the Year during his first spell with Tottenham. He was also German Footballer of the Year in 1988 and 1994.

HENRIK **LARSSON**

Position: Striker
Birth date: September 20, 1971
Birth place: Helsingborg, Sweden
Height: 1.78m (5ft 10in)
Clubs: Hogaborg, Helsingborg, Feyenoord, Celtic, Barcelona, Helsingborg, Manchester United (loan)
International: Sweden (106 caps, 37 goals)
Pro career: 1988-09
It's a fact: Larsson won four Scottish Premier League titles, two Scottish Cups and two Scottish League Cups; two La Liga titles, the Spanish Cup and a Champions League; a Premier League medal; and a Swedish Cup!

BRIAN **LAUDRUP**

Position: Forward
Birth date: February 22, 1969
Birth place: Vienna, Austria
Height: 1.86m (6ft 1in)
Clubs: Brondby, Bayer Uerdingen, Bayern Munich, Fiorentina, AC Milan, Rangers, Chelsea, Copenhagen, Ajax
International: Denmark (82 caps, 21 goals)
Pro career: 1986-00
It's a fact: Laudrup won three Scottish Premier Leagues plus the titles in Denmark and Italy. Four times Denmark Player of the Year, he took the Champions League with Milan plus cups in Germany, Scotland and England.

MICHAEL **LAUDRUP**

Position: Midfielder
Birth date: June 15, 1964
Birth place: Frederiksberg, Denmark
Height: 1.83m (6ft)
Clubs: KB, Brondby, Juventus, Lazio (loan), Barcelona, Real Madrid, Vissel Kobe, Ajax
International: Denmark (104 caps, 37 goals)
Pro career: 1981-98
It's a fact: Voted as Denmark's best-ever player, Laudrup won Serie A with Juventus; La Liga four times with Barcelona and once with Real Madrid; the Eredivisie with Ajax plus the European Cup with Barca.

DENIS **LAW**

Position: Striker
Birth date: February 24, 1940
Birth place: Aberdeen
Height: 1.75m (5ft 9in)
Clubs: Huddersfield, Manchester City, Torino, Manchester United, Manchester City
International: Scotland (55 caps, 30 goals)
Pro career: 1956-74
It's a fact: Law set a British record transfer when he moved from Huddersfield to Man City for £55,000. He was European Footballer of the Year in 1964 and is Scotland's joint record goal-scorer.

GARY **LINEKER**

Position: Striker
Birth date: November 30, 1960
Birth place: Leicester
Height: 1.77m (5ft 9in)
Clubs: Leicester City, Everton, Barcelona, Tottenham, Nagoya Grampus Eight
International: England (80 caps, 48 goals)
Pro career: 1978-94
It's a fact: Lineker is England's second-top scorer ever and their best at World Cup finals with ten goals, including the Golden Boot at the 1986 finals where he hit six. A European Cup and Copa del Rey victor with Barcelona and an FA Cup winner with Tottenham.

DIEGO **MARADONA**

Position: Forward
Birth date: October 31, 1960
Birth place: Buenos Aires, Argentina
Height: 1.65m (5ft 5in)
Clubs: Argentinos Juniors, Boca Juniors, Barcelona, Napoli, Sevilla, Newell's Old Boys, Boca Juniors
International: Argentina (91 games, 34 goals)
Pro career: 1976-97
It's a fact: Twice a world record transfer maker (£5m to Barcelona in 1982 and £6.9m to Napoli in 1984), Maradona is infamous for the "Hand of God" goal against England at the 1986 World Cup.

LOTHAR **MATTHAUS**

Position: Midfielder
Birth date: March 21, 1961
Birth place: Erlangen, Germany
Height: 1.74m (5ft 9in)
Clubs: Borussia Monchengladbach, Bayern Munich, Inter Milan, Bayern Munich, MetroStars
International: Germany (150 caps, 23 goals)
Pro career: 1979-00
It's a fact: Ballon d'Or winner in 1990, Matthaus was World Player of the Year in 1991. He won seven Bundesliga titles with Bayern and Serie A with Inter. He was a World Cup winner in 1990 and European Championship victor in 1980.

STANLEY **MATTHEWS**

Position: Striker
Birth date: February 1, 195
Birth place: Stoke-on-Trent
Height: 1.74m (5ft 9in)
Clubs: Stoke City, Blackpool, Stoke City
International: England (54 caps, 11 goals)
Pro career: 1932-65
It's a fact: Sir Stanley, who died in 2000 at the age of 85, was the first European Footballer or the Year and Football Writers' Footballer of the Year. At the age of 42 years and 104 days he became the oldest player to represent England and in 1965 he was knighted whilst still playing for Stoke.

JACKIE **MILBURN**

Position: Striker
Birth date: May 11, 1924
Birth place: Ashington, Northumberland
Height: 1.82m (6ft)
Clubs: Newcastle United, Linfield
International: England (13 caps, 10 goals)
Pro career: 1943-60
It's a fact: Milburn was Newcastle's all-time top scorer with 200 league goals until Alan Shearer overtook him in 2006 with 206. The main stand at St. James' Park is named after Milburn and there is a statue of him in the city and in his home town. Died in 1988 at the age of 64.

BOBBY **MOORE**

Position: Defender
Birth date: April 12, 1941
Birth place: Barking, Essex
Height: 1.87m (6ft 2in)
Clubs: West Ham, Fulham, San Antonio Thunder, Seattle Sounders, Herning Fremad
International: England (108 caps, 2 goals)
Pro career: 1958-78
It's a fact: Moore, who died in 1993 at the age of 51, was captain of England when the team won the 1966 World Cup on home soil. A statue of him stands outside the main entrance to the new Wembley Stadium.

GERD **MULLER**

Position: Striker
Birth date: November 3, 1945
Birth place: Nordlingen, Germany
Height: 1.76m (5ft 9in)
Clubs: Nordlingen, Bayern Munich, Ford Lauderdale Strikers
International: Germany (62 caps, 68 goals)
Pro career: 1963-81
It's a fact: Muller's international strikes are a German record. He also hit 364 goals in 427 Bundesliga games and 66 in 74 European matches. Four titles, four German Cups and three European Cups with Bayern plus a World Cup and European Championship with his country.

GARY **NEVILLE**

Position: Defender
Birth date: February 18, 1975
Birth place: Bury, Manchester
Height: 1.8m (5ft 11in)
Club: Manchester United
International: England (85 caps, 0 goals)
Pro career: 1992-11
It's a fact: Neville is England's most-capped right back and also made 602 appearances for United between 1992 and 2011. Won eight Premier League titles at Old Trafford, plus three FA Cups, two League Cups, a European Cup, an Intercontinental Cup and Club World Cup.

RUUD **VAN NISTELROOY**

Position: Striker
Birth date: July 1, 1976
Birth place: North Brabant, Holland
Height: 1.88m (6ft 2in)
Clubs: Den Bosch, Heerenveen, PSV Eindhoven, Manchester United, Real Madrid, Hamburg, Malaga
International: Holland (70 games 35 goals)
Pro career: 1993-12
It's a fact: The Dutchman won the league titles in Holland (twice), England (1) and Spain (2) and has been top scorer in both the Eredivisie and Premier League. Three-times the top scorer in the Champions League.

STUART **PEARCE**

Position: Defender
Birth date: April 24, 1962
Birth place: Hammersmith, London
Height: 1.78m (5ft 10in)
Clubs: Coventry City, Nottingham Forest, Newcastle United, West Ham, Manchester City
International: England (78 games, 5 goals)
Pro career: 1978-02
It's a fact: Nicknamed 'Psycho' for his total commitment to the game, Pearce would go on to manage Forest, Man City, England Under-21s and Team GB, and act as interim international manager.

PELE

Position: Forward
Birth date: October 21, 1940
Birth place: Tres Coracoes, Brazil
Height: 1.73m (5ft 8in)
Clubs: Santos, New York Cosmos
International: Brazil (92 caps, 77 goals)
Pro career: 1956-77
It's a fact: Pele is regarded as one of the best players ever with a staggering return of 1,033 goals in 1,120 club appearances. Three times a World Cup-winner, Pele won ten Brazil titles with Santos plus two Copa Libertadores. He was also the top scorer in Brazil's top division for 11 season.

MICHEL **PLATINI**

Position: Midfielder
Birth date: June 21, 1955
Birth place: Joeuf, France
Height: 1.78m (5ft 10in)
Clubs: Nancy, Saint Etienne, Juventus
International: France (72 caps, 41 goals)
Pro career: 1972-87
It's a fact: Platini, now UEFA president, won the 1984 European Championships with France. He was their top scorer and Player of the Tournament. The 1984 European Footballer of the Year was also a twice winner of both the Ballon d'Or and French Player of the Year.

FERENC **PUSKAS**

Position: Midfielder
Birth date: April 1, 1927
Birth place: Budapest, Hungary
Height: 1.69m (5ft 7in)
Clubs: Kispet, Budapest Honved, Real Madrid
International: Hungary (85 caps, 84 goals)
Pro career: 1943-66
It's a fact: Puskas died in 2006 at the age of 79 but left behind an incredible scoring record. His club tally was 616 goals in 620 games. He was a five times winner of both the Hungarian league and La Liga. He was also lifted the European Cup three times with Madrid.

NIALL **QUINN**

Position: Striker
Birth date: October 6, 1966
Birth place: Dublin
Height: 1.93m (6ft 4in)
Clubs: Arsenal, Manchester City, Sunderland
International: Republic of Ireland (92 caps, 21 goals)
Pro career: 1983-02
It's a fact: After hanging up his boots Quinn became chairman of Sunderland from 2006-12. He was the Republic's top scorer until his record was beaten by Robbie Keane in 2004. Quinn won the League Cup with Arsenal and helped Sunderland to promotion to the Premier League.

BRYAN **ROBSON**

Position: Midfielder
Birth date: January 11, 1957
Birth place: Chester-le-Street, Durham
Height: 1.8m (5ft 11in)
Clubs: West Brom, Manchester United, Middlesbrough
International: England (90 caps, 26 goals)
Pro career: 1974-97
It's a fact: Robbo cost United a then British record £1.5m when they bought him from West Brom in 1981. Nicknamed Captain Marvel, he won two Premier League titles, three FA Cups, a League Cup, Cup Winners' Cup and UEFA Super Cup with United. Took Middlesbrough to the Premier League.

RONALDINHO

Position: Forward
Birth date: March 21, 1980
Birth place: Porto Alegre, Brazil
Height: 1.81m (5ft 11in)
Clubs: Gremio, Paris Saint Germain, Barcelona, AC Milan, Flamengo, Athletico Mineiro
International: Brazil (94 games, 33 goals)
Pro career: 1998-present
It's a fact: The twice World Player of the Year has lifted the World Cup and Copa America with his country. He won two La Liga titles, the Champions League and Spanish Super Cup with Barcelona. At AC Milan he won Serie A.

RONALDO

Position: Striker
Birth date: September 22, 1976
Birth place: Rio de Janeiro, Brazil
Height: 1.83m (6ft)
Clubs: Cruzeiro, PSV Eindhoven, Barcelona, Inter Milan, Real Madrid, AC Milan, Corinthians
International: Brazil (98 caps, 62 goals)
Pro career: 1993-11
It's a fact: Three times World Player of the Year, Ronaldo has scored a record 15 goals at World Cup finals. World Cup winner in 1994 and 2002. Two La Ligas with Real Madrid. Lifted the Spanish Super Cup with Madrid and Barca.

IAN **RUSH**

Position: Striker
Birth date: October 20, 1961
Birth place: Flint, Wales
Height: 1.8m (5ft 11in)
Clubs: Chester City, Liverpool, Juventus, Liverpool, Leeds United, Newcastle United, Sheffield United (loan), Wrexham, Sydney Olympic
International: Wales (73 caps, 28 goals)
Pro career: 1978-00
It's a fact: Rush is Wales' and Liverpool's record scorer. His Anfield total is 346, 229 in the league. He was the club's top scorer in nine seasons. Whilst at Anfield, Rush wons five titles, three FA Cups, five League Cups and the European Cup.

PETER **SCHMEICHEL**

Position: Keeper
Birth date: November 18, 1963
Birth place: Gladsaxe, Denmark
Height: 1.91m (6ft 3in)
Clubs: Brondby, Manchester United, Sporting Lisbon, Aston Villa, Manchester City
International: Denmark (129 games, 1 goal)
Pro career: 1987-03
It's a fact: Voted the World's best goalkeeper in 1992 and 1993, Schmeichel lifted five Premier League titles with Man United, including the Treble of league, FA Cup and European Cup in 1999. He scored four goals in his professional career.

ALAN **SHEARER**

Position: Striker
Birth date: August 13, 1970
Birth place: Newcastle
Height: 1.83m (6ft)
Clubs: Southampton, Blackburn Rovers, Newcastle United
International: England (63 games, 30 goals)
Pro career: 1988-06
It's a fact: Shearer, a world record £15m buy from Blackburn by Newcastle in 1996, is the Premier League's record scorer with 260 goals. He's also Newcastle's top scorer. A Premier League winner with Blackburn and twice PFA Players' Player of the Year, plus a FWA Footballer of the Year award.

TEDDY **SHERINGHAM**

Position: Striker
Birth date: April 2, 1966
Birth place: London
Height: 1.83m (6ft)
Clubs: Millwall, Aldershot (loan), Djurgardens (loan), Nottingham Forest, Tottenham, Manchester United, Tottenham, Portsmouth, West Ham, Colchester United
International: England (51 caps, 11 goals)
Pro career: 1983-08
It's a fact: Sheringham was 42 when he retired in 2008 with 354 goals in 898 club fixtures. Three titles, an FA Cup and European Cup with United.

PETER **SHILTON**

Position: Keeper
Birth date: September 18, 1949
Birth place: Leicester
Height: 1.85m (6ft 1in)
Clubs: Leicester City, Stoke City, Nottingham Forest, Southampton, Derby County, Plymouth, Wimbledon, Bolton, Coventry City, West Ham, Leyton Orient
International: England (125 caps, 0 goals)
Pro career: 1966-97
It's a fact: Shilton is England's most-capped player and represented his clubs in a total of 1,237 league and cup games. A league title, League Cup and double European Cup winner with Forest.

SOCRATES

Position: Midfielder
Birth date: February 19, 1954
Birth place: Belem do Para, Brazil
Height: 1.93m (6ft 4in)
Clubs: Botafogo, Corinthians, Fiorentina, Flamengo, Santos, Botafogo
International: Brazil (60 caps, 22 goals)
Pro career: 1974-89
It's a fact: The 1983 South American Footballer of the Year died in 2011 at the age of just 57. He appeared for Brazil at the 1982 and 1986 World Cup finals. Captained the Brazil side of 1982, widely regarded as their best team never to win a World Cup.

NEVILLE **SOUTHALL**

Position: Keeper
Birth date: September 16, 1958
Birth place: Llandudno, Wales
Height: 1.85m (6ft 1in)
Clubs: Bury, Everton, Port Vale (loan), Southend (loan), Stoke City, Torquay United, Huddersfield Town (loan), Bradford City, York City, Shrewsbury Town, Dover Athletic, Dagenham and Redbridge
International: Wales (92 caps, 0 goals)
Pro career: 1980-02
It's a fact: The 1985 FWA Footballer of the Year is the record appearance maker for Wales. He turned out a record 578 league games for Everton.

NOBBY **STILES**

Position: Midfielder
Birth date: May 18, 1942
Birth place: Manchester
Height: 1.68m (5ft 6in)
Clubs: Manchester United, Middlesbrough, Preston North End
International: England (28 caps, 1 goal)
Pro career: 1960-75
It's a fact: Stiles played every minute of England's successful World Cup tournament on home soil in 1966. Famed for his dance with the trophy after the Three Lions' victory. He won three league titles with United, along with one FA Cup, two Charity Shields and the European Cup in 1968.

LILIAN **THURAM**

Position: Defender
Birth date: January 1, 1972
Birth place: Pointe-a-Pitre, Guadeloupe
Height: 1.82m (5ft 11in)
Clubs: Monaco, Parma, Juventus, Barcelona
International: France (142 caps, 2 goals)
Pro career: 1990-08)
It's a fact: Thuram is France's most-capped player and a winner at World Cup 1998 and Euro 2000. He won two Serie A and the Italian Super Cup with Juventus; Spanish Cup at Barcelona; Italy Cup, Italian Super Cup and UEFA Cup at Parma and the French Cup during his time at Monaco.

FRANCESCO **TOTTI**

Position: Midfielder
Birth date: September 27, 1976
Birth place: Rome
Height: 1.8m (5ft 11in)
Club: Roma
International: Italy (58 games, 9 goals)
Pro career: 1992-present
It's a fact: Roma captain Totti can also play as a lone striker and is the club's record goalscorer. He is in the top five Serie A scorers of all-time with more than 200 goals so far. A World Cup-winner in 2006, he also has a Serie A medal and has twice won both Italy's Cup and Super Cup.

BERT **TRAUTMANN**

Position: Keeper
Birth date: October 22, 1923
Birth place: Bremen, Germany
Height: 1.89m (6ft 2in)
Clubs: Manchester City, Wellington Town
International: n/a
Pro career: 1949-64
It's a fact: A German paratrooper captured during the Second World War, Trautmann stayed in England after his release and was signed by Man City. He went on to make 545 appearances for the club and was Football Writers' Footballer of the Year in 1956. Played in a cup final despite a broken neck!

PATRICK **VIEIRA**

Position: Midfielder
Birth date: June 23, 1976
Birth place: Dakar, Senegal
Height: 1.93m (6ft 4in)
Clubs: Cannes, AC Milan, Arsenal, Juventus, Inter Milan, Manchester City
International: France (107 games, 6 goals)
Pro career: 1993-11
It's a fact: The battling midfielder won three Premier Leagues with Arsenal plus the World Cup 1998 and 2000 European Championships with France. Lifted the Italian Super Cup twice and four Serie A titles with Inter plus the FA Cup during his one playing season with Manchester City.

CHRIS **WADDLE**

Position: Winger
Birth date: December 14, 1960
Birth place: Gateshead
Height: 1.88m (6ft 2in)
Clubs: Newcastle United, Tottenham, Marseille, Sheffield Wednesday, Falkirk, Bradford City, Sunderland, Burnley, Torquay United
International: England (62 games, 6 goals)
Pro career: 1980-98
It's a fact: Marseille bought Waddle from Spurs for £4.5m in summer 1989 and he helped them to three consecutive French titles. The 1993 FWA Footballer of the Year during his time at Sheffield Wednesday.

GEORGE **WEAH**

Position: Striker
Birth date: October 1, 1966
Birth place: Monrovia, Liberia
Height: 1.84m (6ft)
Clubs: Monaco, Paris Saint Germain, AC Milan, Chelsea (loan), Manchester City, Marseille, Al-Jazira
International: Liberia (60 games, 22 goals)
Pro career: 1988-03
It's a fact: The 1995 World and European Player of the Year, and African Player of the Year in 1989, 1994 and 1995. Twice a Serie A winner with AC Milan, he won the FA Cup at Chelsea and Ligue 1 with Paris Saint Germain.

BILLY **WRIGHT**

Position: Defender
Birth date: February 6, 1924
Birth place: Ironbridge, Shropshire
Height: 1.73m (5ft 8in)
Club: Wolverhampton Wanderers
International: England (105 caps, 3 goals)
Pro career: 1939-59
It's a fact: Wright was the first player in the world to win more than 100 caps and captained England a record 90 times. He helped Wolves to three league titles and an FA Cup. The 1952 FWA Footballer of the Year and 1957 Ballon D'Or runner-up died in 1994 at the age of 70.

IAN **WRIGHT**

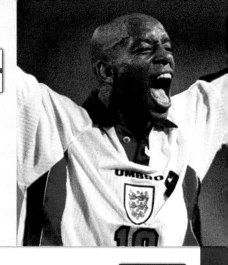

Position: Striker
Birth date: November 3, 1963
Birth place: Woolwich, London
Height: 1.75m (5ft 9in)
Clubs: Crystal Palace, Arsenal, West Ham, Celtic, Burnley
International: England (33 caps, 9 goals)
Pro career: 1985-00
It's a fact: Wright scored a club record 185 goals in 288 games for Arsenal. This was later beaten by Thierry Henry in 2005. He was 34 when he won a Premier League and FA Cup Double with the Gunners, plus a Cup Winners' Cup and League Cup. Division One Golden Boot winner in 1992

LEV **YASHIN**

Position: Keeper
Birth date: October 22, 1923
Birth place: Moscow
Height: 1.89m (6ft 2in)
Clubs: Dynamo Moscow
International: Soviet Union (78 caps, 0 goals)
Pro career: 1950-70
It's a fact: The "Black Spider" is often regarded as football's best-ever keeper. He turned out in more than 800 games, kept 270 clean sheets and is believed to have saved more than 150 penalties. Won five Russian titles plus an Olympic Gold medal and European Championships with his country.

ZINEDINE **ZIDANE**

Position: Midfielder
Birth date: June 23, 1972
Birth place: Marseille, France
Height: 1.85m (6ft 1in)
Clubs: Cannes, Bordeaux, Juventus, Real Madrid
International: France
Pro career: 1988-06
It's a fact: Zidane's last-ever professional game was the 2006 World Cup Final when he captained his country against Italy but got sent-off for a head butt on Marco Materazzi. A World Cup-winner in 1998, European Championship in 2000, plus two titles in Italy and one in Spain.

GIANFRANCO **ZOLA**

Position: Striker
Birth date: July 5, 1966
Birth place: Oliena, Italy
Height: 1.68m (5ft 6in)
Clubs: Nuorese, Torres, Napoli, Parma, Chelsea, Cagliari
International: Italy
Pro career: 1984-05
It's a fact: The 1997 FWA Player of the Year was voted by Chelsea fans as the club's greatest-ever player. Won Serie A and Italian Super Cup with Napoli; UEFA Cup and Super Cup at Parma; two FA Cups, a League Cup, Cup Winners' Cup and UEFA Super Cup during his time at Stamford Bridge.

Pele's 125 Greatest Players

In 2004 the legendary Pele – accepted by many as the greatest footballer ever – compiled a list of 125 top players.

The Brazilian, nominated by FIFA as their Player of the Century, was asked to come up with the names as part of the centenary celebrations of world football's governing body. These were his choices...

Pele

Abedi Pele Ghana
Alan Shearer England
Alessandro Del Piero Italy
Alessandro Nesta Italy
Alfredo Di Stefano Argentina
Andriy Shevchenko Ukraine
Bobby Charlton England
Brian Laudrup Denmark
Cafu Brazil
Carlos Alberto Brazil
Carlos Valderrama Colombia
Christian Vieri Italy
Clarence Seedorf Holland
Daniel Passarella Argentina
David Beckham England
David Trezeguet France
Davor Suker Croatia
Dennis Bergkamp Holland
Didier Deschamps France
Diego Maradona Argentina
Dino Zoff Italy
Djalma Brazil
Edgar Davids Holland
El-Hadji Diouf Senegal
Emilio Butragueno Spain
Emre Belozoglu Turkey
Enzo Francescoli Uruguay
Eric Cantona France
Eusebio Portugal
Falcao Brazil
Ferenc Puskas Hungary
Francesco Totti Italy
Franco Baresi Italy
Frank Rijkaard Holland
Franky van der Elst Belgium
Franz Beckenbauer Germany
Gabriel Batistuta Argentina
Gary Lineker England

George Best

George Best Northern Ireland
George Weah Liberia
Gerd Mueller Germany
Gheorghe Hagi Romania
Giacinto Fachetti Italy
Giampiero Boniperti Italy
Gianluca Buffon Italy
Gianni Rivera Italy
Giuseppe Bergomi Italy
Gordon Banks England
Hernan Crespo Argentina
Hidetoshi Nakata Japan
Hong Myung-Bo South Korea
Hristo Stoichkov Bulgaria
Hugo Sanchez Mexico
Ivan Zamorano Chile
Jan Cuelemans Belgium
Javier Saviola Argentina
Javier Zanetti Argentina
Jay-Jay Okocha Nigeria
Jean-Marie Pfaff Belgium
Jean-Pierre Papin France
Johan Cruyff Holland
Johan Neeskens Holland
Josef Masopust
Czech Republic
Juan Sebastian Veron
Argentina
Junior Brazil

Jurgen Klinsmann Germany
Just Fontaine France
Karl-Heinz Rummenigge
Germany
Kenny Dalglish Scotland
Kevin Keegan England
Lilian Thuram France
Lothar Matthaeus Germany
Luis Enrique Spain
Luis Figo Portugal
Marcel Desailly France
Marco van Basten Holland
Mario Kempes Argentina
Marius Tresor France
Mia Hamm United States
Michael Ballack Germany
Michael Laudrup Denmark
Michael Owen England
Michel Platini France
Michelle Akers United States
Nilton Santos Brazil
Oliver Kahn Germany
Omar Sivori Argentina
Pablo Figueroa Chile
Paolo Maldini Italy
Paolo Rossi Italy
Patrick Kluivert Holland
Patrick Vieira France
Paul Breitner Germany

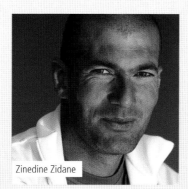
Zinedine Zidane

Pavel Nedved
Czech Repbulic
Pele Brazil
Peter Schmeichel Denmark
Raul Spain
Raymond Kopa France
Rene van de Kerkhof
Holland
Rinat Disayev Russia
Rivaldo Brazil
Rivelino Brazil
Rob Rensenbrink Holland
Robert Pires France
Roberto Baggio Italy
Roberto Carlos Brazil
Roger Milla Cameroon
Romario Brazil
Romerito Paraguay
Ronaldinho Brazil
Ronaldo Brazil
Roy Keane
Republic of Ireland
Rui Costa Portugal
Rustu Recber Turkey
Ruud Gullit Holland
Ruud van Nistelrooy
Holland
Sepp Maier Germany
Socrates Brazil
Teofilo Cubillas Peru
Thierry Henry France
Uwe Seeler Germany
Willie van de Kerkhof
Holland
Zbigniew Boniek
Poland
Zico Brazil
Zinedine Zidane France

PELE FACT FILE

Full name: Edison Arantes do Nascimento
Position: Forward
Birth date: Oct 23, 1940
Birth place: Três Corações, Brazil
Clubs: Santos, New York Cosmos (656 games, 643 goals)
International: Brazil (92 caps, 77 goals)
Did you know? Including all club fixtures, such as friendlies, Pele is said to have played 1,120 games and scored 1,033 goals.

THE
COMPETITIONS

YOUR **GUIDE** TO FOOTBALL **SILVERWARE**
IN **EUROPE** AND **AROUND THE WORLD**

THE FA CUP

The world's oldest and most respected domestic knockout competition began in 1871-72 with just 15 sides.

A crowd of 2,000 attended the first final in which the Wanderers beat the Royal Engineers 1-0 at Kennington Oval.

In season 2011-12 some 763 teams entered and the final between Chelsea and Liverpool attracted a crowd of 90,000 to the new Wembley Stadium.

The extra preliminary rounds for 2011-12 began way back in August 2011 and there were four more sets of qualifiers before the first round proper when teams from League One and Two entered the competition.

The third round – as always – sees the entry of teams from the Premier League and Championship in the draw bag with the games traditionally played on the first Saturday in January.

After that round there are two more before the last eight reach the quarter-finals, then the semi-finals and final. Semis have been played in recent years at Wembley in order to give more fans the chance to see the games live.

The first final at Wembley was in 1923. Between 2001 and 2006 the final was staged at the Millennium Stadium in Cardiff but returned to Wembley in 2007, after the London stadium was rebuilt.

ALL THE WINNERS...

1872 Wanderers 1 Royal Engineers 0
1873 Wanderers 2 Oxford University 0
1874 Oxford University 2 Royal Engineers 0
1875 Royal Engineers 1 Old Etonians 1
(replay Royal Engineers 2 Old Etonians 0)
1876 Wanderers 1 Old Etonians 1
(replay Wanderers 3 Old Etonians 0
1877 Wanderers 2 Oxford University 1 aet
1878 Wanderers 3 Royal Engineers 1
1879 Old Etonians 1 Clapham Rovers 0
1880 Clapham Rovers 1 Oxford University 0
1881 Old Carthusians 3 Old Etonians 0
1882 Old Etonians 1 Blackburn Rovers 0
1883 Blackburn Olympic 2 Old Etonians 1 aet
1884 Blackburn Rovers 2
 Queens Park, Glasgow 1
1885 Blackburn Rovers 2
 Queens Park, Glasgow 0
1886 Blackburn Rovers 0 West Brom 0
 (replay Bburn Rovers 2 West Brom 0)
1887 Aston Villa 2 West Bromwich Albion 0
1888 West Brom 2 Preston North End 1

1920

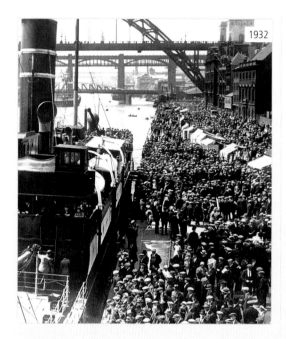

1932

1889 Preston North End 3
Wolverhampton Wanderers 0
1890 Blackburn Rovers 6 The Wednesday 1
1891 Blackburn Rovers 3 Notts County 1
1892 West Bromwich Albion 3 Aston Villa 0
1893 Wolverhampton Wanderers 1 Everton 0
1894 Notts County 4 Bolton Wanderers 1
1895 Aston Villa 1 West Bromwich Albion 0
1896 The Wednesday 2
Wolverhampton Wanderers 1
1897 Aston Villa 3 Everton 2
1898 Nottingham Forest 3 Derby County 1
1899 Sheffield United 4 Derby County 1
1900 Bury 4 Southampton 0
1901 Tottenham Hotspur 2 Sheffield United 2
*(replay Tottenham Hotspur 3
Sheffield United 1)*
1902 Sheffield United 1 Southampton 1
(replay Sheffield United 2 Southampton 1)
1903 Bury 6 Derby County 0

1904 Manchester City 1 Bolton Wanderers 0
1905 Aston Villa 2 Newcastle United 0
1906 Everton 1 Newcastle United 0
1907 The Wednesday 2 Everton 1
1908 Wolverhampton Wanderers 3
Newcastle United 1
1909 Manchester United 1 Bristol City 0
1910 Newcastle United 1 Barnsley 1
(replay Newcastle United 2 Barnsley 0)
1911 Bradford City 0 Newcastle United 0
(replay Bradford City 1 Newcastle United 0)
1912 Barnsley 0 West Bromwich Albion 0
(replay Barnsley 1 West Bromwich Albion 0)
1913 Aston Villa 1 Sunderland 0
1914 Burnley 1 Liverpool 0
1915 Sheffield United 3 Chelsea 0
No competition due to First World War
1920 Aston Villa 1 Huddersfield Town 0 aet
1921 Tottenham Hotspur 1
Wolverhampton Wanderers 0

1960

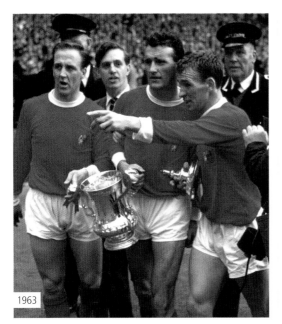

1963

1946 Derby County 4 Charlton Athletic 1 aet
1947 Charlton Athletic 1 Burnley 0 aet
1948 Manchester United 4 Blackpool 2
1949 Wolverhampton Wanderers 3 Leicester City 1
1950 Arsenal 2 Liverpool 0
1951 Newcastle United 2 Blackpool 0
1952 Newcastle United 1 Arsenal 0
1953 Blackpool 4 Bolton Wanderers 3
1954 West Bromwich Albion 3
Preston North End 2
1955 Newcastle United 3 Manchester City 1
1956 Manchester City 3 Birmingham City 1
1957 Aston Villa 2 Manchester United 1
1958 Bolton Wanderers 2 Manchester United 0
1959 Nottingham Forest 2 Luton Town 1
1960 Wolverhampton Wanderers 3
Blackburn Rovers 0
1961 Tottenham Hotspur 2 Leicester City 0
1962 Tottenham Hotspur 3 Burnley 1
1963 Manchester United 3 Leicester City 1

1922 Huddersfield Town 1 Preston North End 0
1923 Bolton Wanderers 2 West Ham United 0
1924 Newcastle United 2 Aston Villa 0
1925 Sheffield United 1 Cardiff City 0
1926 Bolton Wanderers 1 Manchester City 0
1927 Cardiff City 1 Arsenal 0
1928 Blackburn Rovers 3 Huddersfield Town 1
1929 Bolton Wanderers 2 Portsmouth 0
1930 Arsenal 2 Huddersfield Town 0
1931 West Bromwich Albion 2 Birmingham City 1
1932 Newcastle United 2 Arsenal 1
1933 Everton 3 Manchester City 0
1934 Manchester City 2 Portsmouth 1
1935 Sheffield Wednesday 4
West Bromwich Albion 2
1936 Arsenal 1 Sheffield United 0
1937 Sunderland 3 Preston North End 1
1938 Preston North End 1 Huddersfield Town 0 aet
1939 Portsmouth 4 Wolverhampton Wanderers 1
No competition due to Second World War

1970

1981

1964 West Ham United 3 Preston North End 2
1965 Liverpool 2 Leeds United 1 aet
1966 Everton 3 Sheffield Wednesday 2
1967 Tottenham Hotspur 2 Chelsea 1
1968 West Bromwich Albion 1 Everton 0 aet
1969 Manchester City 1 Leicester City 0
1970 Chelsea 2 Leeds United 2
(replay Chelsea 2 Leeds United 1)
1971 Arsenal 2 Liverpool 1 aet
1972 Leeds United 1 Arsenal 0
1973 Sunderland 1 Leeds United 0
1974 Liverpool 3 Newcastle United 0
1975 West Ham United 2 Fulham 0
1976 Southampton 1 Manchester United 0
1977 Manchester United 2 Liverpool 1
1978 Ipswich Town 1 Arsenal 0
1979 Arsenal 3 Manchester United 2
1980 West Ham United 1 Arsenal 0
1981 Tottenham Hotspur 1 Manchester City 1
*(replay Tottenham Hotspur 3
Manchester City 2)*

1982 Tottenham Hotspur 1 Queens Park Rangers 1
*(replay Tottenham Hotspur 1
Queens Park Rangers 0)*
1983 Manchester United 2
Brighton and Hove Albion 2
*(replay Manchester United 4
Brighton and Hove Albion 0)*
1984 Everton 2 Watford 0
1985 Manchester United 1 Everton 0 aet
1986 Liverpool 3 Everton 1
1987 Coventry City 3 Tottenham Hotspur 2 aet
1988 Wimbledon 1 Liverpool 0
1989 Liverpool 3 Everton 2 aet
1990 Manchester United 3 Crystal Palace 3
*(replay Manchester United 1
Crystal Palace 0)*
1991 Tottenham Hotspur 2
Nottingham Forest 1 aet
1992 Liverpool 2 Sunderland 0
1993 Arsenal 1 Sheffield Wednesday 1
(replay Arsenal 2 Sheffield Wednesday 1 aet)

1989

2001

2012

1994 Manchester United 4 Chelsea 0
1995 Everton 1 Manchester United 0
1996 Manchester United 1 Liverpool 0
1997 Chelsea 2 Middlesbrough 0
1998 Arsenal 2 Newcastle United 0
1999 Manchester United 2 Newcastle United 0
2000 Chelsea 1 Aston Villa 0
2001 Liverpool 2 Arsenal 1
2002 Arsenal 2 Chelsea 0
2003 Arsenal 1 Southampton 0
2004 Manchester United 3 Millwall 0
2005 Arsenal 0 Manchester United 0 aet
   (Arsenal won 5-4 on penalties)
2006 Liverpool 3 West Ham United 3
   (Liverpool won 3-1 on penalties)
2007 Chelsea 1 Manchester United 0 aet
2008 Portsmouth 1 Cardiff City 0
2009 Chelsea 2 Everton 1
2010 Chelsea 1 Portsmouth 0
2011 Manchester City 1 Stoke City 0
2012 Chelsea 2 Liverpool 1

2008

2009

THE LEAGUE CUP

The League Cup is competed for by all 72 English Football League teams plus the 20 sides in the Premier League.

It's often regarded as a secondary event by many top clubs – yet it still carries a ticket to European competition for the winners.

First played in season 1960-61, the League Cup was designated a midweek tournament. It grew in popularity when the winners were granted entry to the UEFA Cup (now Europa League).

During its history sponsorship has seen the trophy called the Milk, Littlewoods, Rumbelows, Coca-Cola, Worthington and now Carling Cup.

For the first six years of the cup's existence the final was a two-legged affair with home and away games. From 1967 onwards it has been a one-off final, played mostly at Wembley.

2010

2011

2012

ALL THE WINNERS...

1961 Aston Villa (0) 3 Rotherham (2) 0 aet
1962 Norwich (3) 1 Rochdale (0) 0
1963 Birmingham City (3) 0 Aston Villa (1) 0
1964 Leicester (1) 3 Stoke City (1) 2
1965 Chelsea (3) 0 Leicester (2) 0
1966 West Brom (1) 4 West Ham (2) 1
1967 QPR 3 West Brom 2
1968 Leeds 1 Arsenal 0
1969 Swindon 3 Arsenal 1 aet
1970 Manchester City 2 West Brom 1 (aet)
1971 Tottenham 2 Aston Villa 0
1972 Stoke City 2 Chelsea 1
1973 Tottenham 1 Norwich City 0
1974 Wolves 2 Manchester City 1
1975 Aston Villa 1 Norwich 0
1976 Manchester City 2 Newcastle 1
1977 Aston Villa 3 Everton 2
 (second replay Old Trafford,
 0-0 Wembley, 1-1 Hillsborough aet)
1978 Nottingham Forest 1 Liverpool 0
 (*replay Old Trafford, 0-0 Wembley*)
1979 Nottingham Forest 3 Southampton 2
1980 Wolves 1 Nottingham Forest 0
1981 Liverpool 2 West Ham 1
 (*replay Villa Park, 1-1 Wembley*)
1982 Liverpool 3 Tottenham 1 aet
1983 Liverpool 2 Manchester United 1 aet
1984 Liverpool 1 Everton 0
 (*replay Maine Road, 0-0 Wembley*)
1985 Norwich 1 Sunderland 0
1986 Oxford United 3 QPR 0
1987 Arsenal 2 Liverpool 1
1988 Luton Town 3 Arsenal 2
1989 Nottingham Forest 3 Luton Town 1
1990 Nottingham Forest 1 Oldham 0
1991 Sheffield Wednesday 1 Manchester United 0
1992 Manchester United 1 Nottingham Forest 0
1993 Arsenal 2 Sheffield Wednesday 1

1994 Aston Villa 3 Manchester United 1
1995 Liverpool 2 Bolton 1
1996 Aston Villa 3 Leeds 0
1997 Leicester 1 Middlesbrough 0
 (*replay at Hillsborough, 1-1 at Wembley*)
1998 Chelsea 2 Middlesbrough 0 aet
1999 Tottenham 1 Leicester 0
2000 Leicester 2 Tranmere 1
2001 Liverpool 1 Birmingham 1
 (*Liverpool 5-4, penalty shoot-out*)
2002 Blackburn 2 Tottenham 1
2003 Liverpool 2 Manchester United 0
2004 Middlesbrough 2 Bolton 1
2005 Chelsea 3 Liverpool 2 aet
2006 Manchester United 4 Wigan 0
2007 Chelsea 2 Arsenal 1
2008 Tottenham 2 Chelsea 1 aet
2009 Manchester United 0 Tottenham 0
 (*United 4-1, penalty shoot-out*)
2010 Manchester United 2 Aston Villa 1
2011 Birmingham City 2 Arsenal 1
2012 Liverpool 2 Cardiff City 2
 (*Liverpool 3-2, penalty shoot-out*)

2012

THE CHARITY/ COMMUNITY SHIELD

O riginally a game between a top professional side and a leading amateur team, the Charity Shield changed its name to the Community Shield in 2003.

Since 1974 it has become a traditional curtain raiser at Wembley between the League and FA Cup winners.

Like the FA Cup, the final was moved to Cardiff's Millennium Stadium during the rebuilding of England's national stadium.

2011

ALL THE WINNERS...

1908 Manchester United 1 Queens Park Rangers 1
(replay Manchester United 4 QPR 0)
1909 Newcastle United 2 Northampton Town 0
1910 Brighton and Hove Albion 1 Aston Villa 0
1911 Manchester United 8 Swindon Town 4
1912 Blackburn Rovers 2 Queens Park Rangers 1
1913 Professionals 7 Amateurs 2
(No competition due to First World War)
1920 West Bromwich Albion 2 Tottenham Hotspur 0
1921 Tottenham Hotspur 2 Burnley 0
1922 Huddersfield Town 1 Liverpool 0
1923 Professionals 2 Amateurs 0
1924 Professionals 3 Amateurs 1
1925 Amateurs 6 Professionals 1
1926 Amateurs 6 Professionals 3
1927 Cardiff City 2 Corinthians 1
1928 Everton 2 Blackburn Rovers 1
1929 Professionals 3 Amateurs 0
1930 Arsenal 2 Sheffield Wednesday 1
1931 Arsenal 1 West Bromwich Albion 0
1932 Everton 5 Newcastle United 3
1933 Arsenal 3 Everton 0
1934 Arsenal 4 Manchester City 0
1935 Sheffield Wednesday 1 Arsenal 0
1936 Sunderland 2 Arsenal 1
1937 Manchester City 2 Sunderland 0
1938 Arsenal 2 Preston North End 1
(No competition due to Second World War)
1948 Arsenal 4 Manchester United 3
1949 Portsmouth 1 Wolverhampton Wanderers 1
(Shared Shield)
1950 World Cup Team 4 Canadian Touring Team 2
1951 Tottenham Hotspur 2 Newcastle United 1
1952 Manchester United 4 Newcastle United 2
1953 Arsenal 3 Blackpool 1
1954 Wolverhampton Wanderers 4 West Brom 4
(Shared Shield)
1955 Chelsea 3 Newcastle United 0

1956 Manchester United 1 Manchester City 0

1957 Manchester United 4 Aston Villa 0

1958 Bolton Wanderers 4 Wolves 1

1959 Wolves 3 Nottingham Forest 1

1960 Burnley 2 Wolves 2
(Shared Shield)

1961 Tottenham Hotspur 3 FA XI 2

1962 Tottenham Hotspur 5 Ipswich Town 1

1963 Everton 4 Manchester United 0

1964 Liverpool 2 West Ham United 2
(Shared Shield)

1965 Manchester United 2 Liverpool 2
(Shared Shield)

1966 Liverpool 1 Everton 0

1967 Manchester United 3 Tottenham Hotspur 3
(Shared Shield)

1968 Manchester City 6 West Bromwich Albion 1

1969 Leeds United 2 Manchester City 1

1970 Everton 2 Chelsea 1

1971 Leicester City 1 Liverpool 0

1972 Manchester City 1 Aston Villa 0

1973 Burnley 1 Manchester City 0

1974 Liverpool 1 Leeds United 1
(Liverpool 6-5 on penalties)

1975 Derby County 2 West Ham United 0

1976 Liverpool 1 Southampton 0

1977 Liverpool 0 Manchester United 0
(Shared Shield)

1978 Nottingham Forest 5 Ipswich Town 0

1979 Liverpool 3 Arsenal 1

1980 Liverpool 1 West Ham United 0

1981 Aston Villa 2 Tottenham Hotspur 2
(Shared Shield)

1982 Liverpool 1 Tottenham Hotspur 0

1983 Manchester United 2 Liverpool 0

1984 Everton 1 Liverpool 0

1985 Everton 2 Manchester United 0

1986 Everton 1 Liverpool 1 *(Shared Shield)*

1987 Everton 1 Coventry City 0

1988 Liverpool 2 Wimbledon 1

1989 Liverpool 1 Arsenal 0

1990 Liverpool 1 Manchester United 1
(Shared Shield)

1991 Arsenal 0 Tottenham Hotspur 0
(Shared Shield)

1992 Leeds United 4 Liverpool 3

1993 Manchester United 1 Arsenal 1
(United 5-4 on penalties)

1994 Manchester United 2 Blackburn Rovers 0

1995 Everton 1 Blackburn Rovers 0

1996 Manchester United 4 Newcastle United 0

1997 Manchester United 1 Chelsea 1
(United 4-2 on penalties)

1998 Arsenal 3 Manchester United 0

1999 Arsenal 2 Manchester United 1

2000 Chelsea 2 Manchester United 0

2001 Liverpool 2 Manchester United 1

2002 Arsenal 1 Liverpool 0

2003 Manchester United 1 Arsenal 1
(United 4-3 on penalties)

2004 Arsenal 3 Manchester United 1

2005 Chelsea 2 Arsenal 1

2006 Liverpool 2 Chelsea 1

2007 Manchester United 1 Chelsea 1
(United 3-0 on penalties)

2008 Manchester United 0 Portsmouth 0
(United 3-1 on penalties)

2009 Chelsea 2 Manchester United 2
(Chelsea 4-1 on penalties)

2010 Manchester United 3 Chelsea 1

2011 Manchester United 3 Manchester City 2

2011

THE EUROPEAN CUP

CHAMPIONS LEAGUE

I t's regarded as the biggest club competition in Europe – and a quick look down the list of past winners illustrates just why!

The former holders of the European Cup reads like a who's who of the continent's biggest and best teams.

Having begun life in 1955-56 as the European Champion Clubs' Cup – shortened to European Cup – the competition became known as the Champions League in 1992.

Originally played on a simple knockout basis, the competition is now run on a group/league stage format before ending in knockout rounds.

ALL THE WINNERS...

1956 Real Madrid 4 Stade de Reims 3
1957 Real Madrid 2 Fiorentina 0
1958 Real Madrid 3 AC Milan 2 aet
1959 Real Madrid 2 Stade de Reims 0
1960 Real Madrid 7 Eintracht Frankfurt 3
1961 Benfica 3 Barcelona 2
1962 Benfica 5 Real Madrid 3
1963 AC Milan 2 Benfica 1
1964 Inter Milan 3 Real Madrid 1
1965 Inter Milan 1 Benfica 0
1966 Real Madrid 2 Partizan 1
1967 Celtic 2 Inter Milan 1
1968 Manchester United 4 Benfica 1 aet
1969 AC Milan 4 Ajax 1
1970 Feyenoord 2 Celtic 1 aet
1971 Ajax 2 Panathinaikos 0
1972 Ajax 2 Inter Milan 0
1973 Ajax 1 Juventus 0
1974 Bayern Munich 4 Atletico Madrid 0
(replay, first game 1-1)
1975 Bayern Munich 2 Leeds United 0
1976 Bayern Munich 1 Saint-Etienne 0

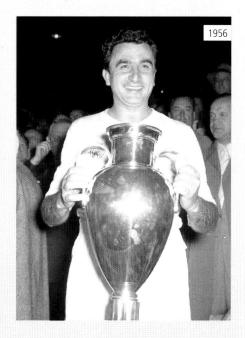

1956

1972

1981

1993

1977 Liverpool 3 Borussia Monchengladbach 1
1978 Liverpool 1 Club Brugge 0
1979 Nottingham Forest 1 Malmo 0
1980 Nottingham Forest 1 Hamburg 0
1981 Liverpool 1 Real Madrid 0
1982 Aston Villa 1 Bayern Munich 0
1983 Hamburg 1 Juventus 0
1984 Liverpool 1 Roma 1
(Liverpool 4-2 on penalties)
1985 Juventus 1 Liverpool 0
1986 Steaua Bucharest 0 Barcelona 0
(Bucharest 2-0 on penalties)
1987 Porto 2 Bayern Munich 1
1988 PSV Eindhoven 0 Benfica 0
(PSV 6-5 on penalties)
1989 AC Milan 4 Steaua Bucharest 0
1990 AC Milan 1 Benfica 0
1991 Red Star Belgrade 0 Marseille 0
(Red Star 5-3 on penalties)
1992 Barcelona 1 Sampdoria 0 aet

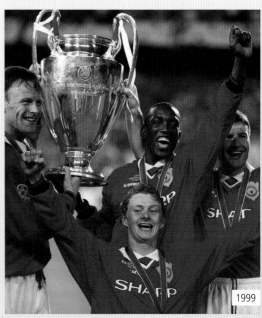

1999

2000

1999 Manchester United 2 Bayern Munich 1
2000 Real Madrid 3 Valencia 0
2001 Bayern Munich 1 Valencia 1
(Bayern 5-4 on penalties)
2002 Real Madrid 2 Bayer Leverkusen 1
2003 AC Milan 0 Juventus 0
(Milan 3-2 on penalties)
2004 Porto 3 Monaco 0
2005 Liverpool 3 AC Milan 3
(Liverpool 3-2 on penalties)
2006 Barcelona 2 Arsenal 1
2007 AC Milan 2 Liverpool 1
2008 Manchester United 1 Chelsea 1
(United 6-5 on penalties)
2009 Barcelona 2 Manchester United 0
2010 Inter Milan 2 Bayern Munich 0
2011 Barcelona 3 Manchester United 1
2012 Bayern Munich 1 Chelsea 1
(Chelsea 4-3 on penalties)

1993 Marseille 1 AC Milan 0
1994 AC Milan 4 Barcelona 0
1995 Ajax 1 AC Milan 0
1996 Juventus 1 Ajax 1
(Juventus 4-2 on penalties)
1997 Borussia Dortmund 3 Juventus 1
1998 Real Madrid 1 Juventus 0

2008

2012

UEFA CUP EUROPA LEAGUE

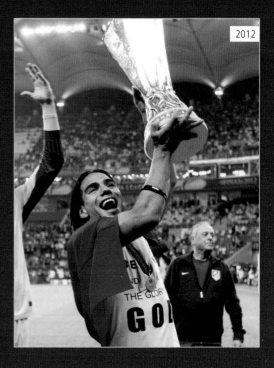

2012

The UEFA Cup ran from 1971-72 until 2009-10 when it became known as the Europa League and changed its format. It is the secondary competition to the European Champions League. Teams qualify for the tournament subject to where they finish in their domestic leagues.

The former Cup Winners' Cup was scrapped in 1999 and the InterToto Cup ceased in 2009, both became part of this UEFA competition. The final was two-legged until 1997. Winners first, aggregate score in brackets.

ALL THE WINNERS...

1972 Tottenham v Wolves (3-2)
1973 Liverpool v B. Monchengladbach (3-2)
1974 Feyenoord v Tottenham (4-2)
1975 B. Monchengladbach v Twente (5-1)
1976 Liverpool v Brugge (4-3)
1977 Juventus v Athletic Bilbao (2-2, away goal)
1978 PSV Eindhoven v Bastia (3-0)
1979 B. Monchengladbach v Red Star (2-1)
1980 Eintracht Frankfurt v B. Monchengladbach (3-3, away goal)
1981 Ipswich Town v AZ Alkmaar (5-4)
1982 IFK Gothenburg v Hamburg (4-0)
1983 Anderlecht v Benfica (2-1)
1984 Tottenham v Anderlecht (2-2, aet, Spurs 4-3 pens)
1985 Real Madrid v Videotron (3-1)
1986 Real Madrid v Cologne (5-3)
1987 IFK Gothenburg v Dundee United (2-1)

2000

1988 Bayer Leverkusen v Espanyol (3-3, aet, Bayer 3-2 pens)
1989 Napoli v Stuttgart (5-4)
1990 Juventus v Fiorentina (3-1)
1991 Inter Milan v Roma (2-1)
1992 Ajax v Torino (2-2, away goal)
1993 Juventus v Borussia Dortmund (6-1)
1994 Inter Milan v Salzburg (2-0)
1995 Parma v Juventus (2-1)
1996 Bayern Munich v Bordeaux (5-1)
1997 Schalke 04 v Inter Milan (1-1, aet, Schalke 4-1 pens)
1998 Inter Milan 3 Lazio 0
1999 Parma 3 Marseille 0
2000 Galatasaray 0 Arsenal 0 (Gala 4-1 pens)
2001 Liverpool 5 Alaves 4 (aet, sudden death)
2002 Feyenoord 3 Borussia Dortmund 2
2003 Porto 3 Celtic 2 (aet)
2004 Valencia 2 Marseille 0
2005 CSKA Moscow 3 Sporting Lisbon 1
2006 Sevilla 4 Middlesbrough 0
2007 Sevilla 2 Espanyol 2 (aet, Sevilla 3-1 pens)
2008 Zenit St. Petersburg 2 Rangers 0
2009 Shakhtar Donetsk 2 Werder Bremen 1
2010 Atletico Madrid 2 Fulham 1 (aet)
2011 Porto 1 Braga 0
2012 Atleticó Madrid 3 Athletic Bilbao 0

1966

INTER-CITIES FAIRS CUP

The Inter-Cities Fairs Cup was the forerunner of the UEFA Cup, but was not organised by European football's governing body. (Two leg scores in brackets)

1958 London 2 Barcelona 8 (2-2, 6-0)*

1960 Birmingham 1 Barcelona 4 (0-0, 4-1) **

1961 Birmingham 2 Roma 4 (2-2, 2-0)

1962 Valencia 7 Barcelona 3 (6-2, 1-1)

1963 Dynamo Zagreb 1 Valencia 4 (1-2, 2-0)

1964 Real Zaragoza 2 Valencia 1

1965 Ferencvaros 1 Juventus 0

1966 Barcelona 4 Zaragoza 3 (0-1, 2-4)

1967 Dynamo Zagreb 2 Leeds 0 (2-0, 0-0)

1968 Leeds United 1 Ferencvaros 0 (1-0, 0-0)

1969 Newcastle United 6 U. Dozsa 2 (3-0, 2-3)

1970 Arsenal 4 Anderlect 3 (3-1, 3-0)

1971 Leeds United 3 Juventus 3 (2-2, 1-1, Leeds won on away goals)

*Ran between 1955-58. Ran between 1959-60

1971

2005

UEFA SUPER CUP

The winners of the Champions League and the Europa League winners meet for the European Super Cup. Previously it was contested by the European Cup and UEFA Cup victors. It is traditionally an opener to the new season.

It was a two-legged event from 1972-1997, but was played as a single tie in 1984, 1986 and 1991 with no games in 1974, 1981 and 1985.

1972 Ajax	**1992** Barcelona
1973 Ajax	**1993** Parma
1974 Not played	**1994** AC Milan
1975 Dynamo Kiev	**1995** Ajax
1976 Anderlecht	**1996** Juventus
1977 Liverpool	**1997** Barcelona
1978 Anderlecht	**1998** Chelsea
1979 Nott'm Forest	**1999** Lazio
1980 Valencia	**2001** Liverpool
1981 Not played	**2002** Real Madrid
1982 Aston Villa	**2003** AC Milan
1983 Aberdeen	**2004** Valencia
1984 Juventus	**2005** Liverpool
1985 Not played	**2006** Sevilla
1986 Steaua Bucharest	**2007** AC Milan
1987 Porto	**2008** Zenit St. Petersburg
1988 Mechelen	
1989 AC Milan	**2009** Barcelona
1990 AC Milan	**2010** Atletico Madrid
1991 Man United	**2011** Barcelona

SPAIN

Founded in 1929, La Liga is Spain's top division and often regarded as one of the top three leagues in the world. Attendances at matches are topped only by clubs in England and Germany.

ALL THE WINNERS...

1929	Barcelona		**1960**	Barcelona
1930	Athletic Bilbao		**1961**	Real Madrid
1931	Athletic Bilbao		**1962**	Real Madrid
1932	Real Madrid		**1963**	Real Madrid
1933	Real Madrid		**1964**	Real Madrid
1934	Athletic Bilbao		**1965**	Real Madrid
1935	Real Betis		**1966**	Atletico Madrid
1936	Athletic Bilbao		**1967**	Real Madrid
1936-39	**Spanish Civil War**		**1968**	Real Madrid
1940	Atletico Aviacion		**1969**	Real Madrid
1941	Atletico Aviacion		**1970**	Atletico Madrid
1942	Valencia		**1971**	Valencia
1943	Athletic Bilbao		**1972**	Real Madrid
1944	Valencia		**1973**	Atletico Madrid
1945	Barcelona		**1974**	Barcelona
1946	Sevilla			
1947	Valencia			
1948	Barcelona			
1949	Barcelona			
1950	Atletico Madrid			
1951	Atletico Madrid			
1952	Barcelona			
1953	Barcelona			
1954	Real Madrid			
1955	Real Madrid			
1956	Athletic Bilbao			
1957	Real Madrid			
1958	Real Madrid			
1959	Barcelona			

2012

1986

1958

1975	Real Madrid		**1989**	Real Madrid
1976	Real Madrid		**1990**	Real Madrid
1977	Atletico Madrid		**1991**	Barcelona
1978	Real Madrid		**1992**	Barcelona
1979	Real Madrid		**1993**	Barcelona
1980	Real Madrid		**1994**	Barcelona
1981	Real Sociedad		**1995**	Real Madrd
1982	Real Sociedad		**1996**	Atletico Madrid
1983	Athletic Bilbao		**1997**	Real Madrid
1984	Athletic Bilbao		**1998**	Barcelona
1985	Barcelona		**1999**	Barcelona
1986	Real Madrid		**2000**	Deportivo La Coruna
1987	Real Madrid		**2001**	Real Madrid
1988	Real Madrid		**2002**	Valencia
			2003	Real Madrid
			2004	Valencia
			2005	Barcelona
			2006	Barcelona
			2007	Real Madrid
			2008	Real Madrid
			2009	Barcelona
			2010	Barcelona
			2011	Barcelona
			2012	Real Madrid

ITALY

2012

Serie A, Italy's highest division, is officially ranked fourth in Europe behind the top leagues in England, Germany and Spain. It was founded in 1898 and ran as a divisional contest before becoming a single league in 1929.

PRIMA CATEGORIA

1898	Genoa
1899	Genoa
1900	Genoa
1901	AC Milan
1902	Genoa
1903	Genoa
1904	Genoa
1905	Juventus
1906	AC Milan
1907	AC Milan
1908	Pro Vercelli
1909	Pro Vercelli
1910	Inter Milan
1911	Pro Vercelli
1912	Pro Vercelli
1913	Pro Vercelli
1914	Casale
1915	Genoa
1916-19	World War I
1920	Inter Milan
1921	Pro Vercelli
1922	Novese

PRIMA DIVISIONE

1922	Pro Vercelli
1923	Genoa
1924	Genoa
1925	Bologna
1926	Juventus

DIVISIONE NAZIONALE

1927	Torino*
1928	Torino
1929	Bologna

*Stripped of title

SERIE A

1930	Inter Milan
1931	Juventus
1932	Juventus
1933	Juventus
1934	Juventus
1935	Juventus
1936	Bologna
1937	Bologna
1938	Inter Milan
1939	Bologna
1940	Inter Milan
1941	Bologna
1942	Roma
1943	Torino
1944-45	World War II
1946	Torino
1947	Torino
1948	Torino
1949	Torino
1950	Juventus
1951	AC Milan
1952	Juventus
1953	Inter Milan
1954	Inter Milan
1955	AC Milan
1956	Fiorentina
1957	AC Milan
1958	Juventus
1959	AC Milan
1960	Juventus
1961	Juventus
1962	AC Milan
1963	Inter Milan
1964	Bologna
1965	Inter Milan
1966	Inter Milan
1967	Juventus
1968	AC Milan
1969	Fiorentina
1970	Cagliari Calcio
1971	Inter Milan
1972	Juventus
1973	Juventus
1974	Lazio
1975	Juventus
1976	Torino
1977	Juventus
1978	Juventus
1979	AC Milan
1980	Inter Milan
1981	Juventus
1982	Juventus
1983	Romas
1984	Juventus
1985	Verona
1986	Juventus
1987	Napoli
1988	AC Milan
1989	Inter Milan
1990	Napoli
1991	Sampdoria
1992	AC Milan
1993	AC Milan
1994	AC Milan
1995	Juventus
1996	AC Milan
1997	Juventus
1998	Juventus
1999	AC Milan
2000	Lazio
2001	Roma
2002	Juventus
2003	Juventus
2004	AC Milan
2005	Juventus*
2006	Inter Milan
2007	Inter Milan
2008	Inter Milan
2009	Inter Milan
2010	Inter Milan
2011	AC Milan
2012	Juventus

*Stripped of title

GERMANY

The Bundesliga is officially ranked third in Europe – but it has enjoyed some of the highest average attendances at games in recent years. It was formed as recently as 1963 and has had a second division since 1974. There is also a third professional league in Germany.

2008

ALL THE WINNERS...

1964 Cologne
1965 Werder Bremen
1966 Munich 1860
1967 Eintracht Braunschweig
1968 Nuremberg
1969 Bayern Munich
1970 Borussia Monchengladbach
1971 Borussia Monchengladbach
1972 Bayern Munich
1973 Bayern Munich
1974 Bayern Munich
1975 Borussia Monchengladbach
1976 Borussia Monchengladbach
1977 Borussia Monchengladbach
1978 Cologne
1979 Hamburg
1980 Bayern Munich
1981 Bayern Munich
1982 Hamburg
1983 Hamburg
1984 Stuttgart
1985 Bayern Munich
1986 Bayern Munich

1987 Bayern Munich
1988 Werder Bremen
1989 Bayern Munich
1990 Bayern Munich
1991 Kaiserslautern
1992 Stuttgart
1993 Werder Bremen
1994 Bayern Munich
1995 Borussia Dortmund
1996 Borussia Dortmund
1997 Bayern Munich
1998 Kaiserslautern
1999 Bayern Munich
2000 Bayern Munich
2001 Bayern Munich
2002 Borussia Dortmund
2003 Bayern Munich
2004 Werder Bremen
2005 Bayern Munich
2006 Bayern Munich
2007 Stuttgart
2008 Bayern Munich
2009 Wolfsburg
2010 Bayern Munich
2011 Borussia Dortmund
2012 Borussia Dortmund

2004

2012

1986

FRANCE

France's first professional league was called the National and ran for season 1932-33. It became Division One to 2002 before taking on its present name of Ligue 1. France has a second division.

ALL THE WINNERS...

1933	Olympique Lillois	**1964**	Saint-Etienne	**1990**	Marseille
1934	Sete	**1965**	Nantes	**1991**	Marseille
1935	Sochaux	**1966**	Nantes	**1992**	Marseille
1936	RCF Paris	**1967**	Saint-Etienne	**1993**	Marseille*
1937	Marseille	**1968**	Saint-Etienne	**1994**	Paris Saint German
1938	Sochaux	**1969**	Saint-Etienne	**1995**	Nantes
1939	Sete	**1970**	Saint-Etienne	**1996**	Auxerre
1940-45	World War II	**1971**	Marseille	**1997**	Monaco
1946	Lille	**1972**	Marseille	**1998**	Lens
1947	Roubaix-Tourcoing	**1973**	Nantes	**1999**	Bordeaux
1948	Marseille	**1974**	Saint-Etienne	**2000**	Monaco
1949	Stade Reims	**1975**	Saint-Etienne	**2001**	Nantes
1950	Bordeaux	**1976**	Saint-Etienne	**2002**	Lyon
1951	Nice	**1977**	Nantes	**2003**	Lyon
1952	Nice	**1978**	Monaco	**2004**	Lyon
1953	Stade Reims	**1979**	Strasbourg	**2005**	Lyon
1954	Lille	**1980**	Nantes	**2006**	Lyon
1955	Stade Reims	**1981**	Saint-Etienne	**2007**	Lyon
1956	Nice	**1982**	Monaco	**2008**	Lyon
1957	Saint-Etienne	**1983**	Nantes	**2009**	Bordeaux
1958	Stade Reims	**1984**	Bordeaux	**2010**	Marseille
1959	Nice	**1985**	Bordeaux	**2011**	Lille
1960	Stade Reims	**1986**	Paris Saint German	**2012**	Montpellier
1961	Monaco	**1987**	Bordeaux	*Stripped of title	
1962	Stade Reims	**1988**	Monaco		
1963	Monaco	**1989**	Marseille		

HOLLAND

Professional football got under way two years before the Eredivisie began in Holland in 1956. The Netherlands also has a first division, the Eerste Divisie.

2012

ALL THE WINNERS…

1957	Ajax	**1965**	Feyenoord		
1958	DOS	**1966**	Ajax		
1959	Sparta	**1967**	Ajax		
1960	Ajax	**1968**	Ajax		
1961	Feyenoord	**1969**	Feyenoord		
1962	Feyenoord	**1970**	Ajax	**1983**	Ajax
1963	PSV Eindhoven	**1971**	Feyenoord	**1984**	Feyenoord
1964	DWS	**1972**	Ajax	**1985**	Ajax
		1973	Ajax	**1986**	PSV Eindhoven
		1974	Feyenoord	**1987**	PSV Eindhoven
		1975	PSV Eindhoven	**1988**	PSV Eindhoven
		1976	PSV Eindhoven	**1989**	PSV Eindhoven
		1977	Ajax	**1990**	Ajax
		1978	PSV Eindhoven	**1991**	PSV Eindhoven
		1979	Ajax	**1992**	PSV Eindhoven
		1980	Ajax	**1993**	Feyenoord
		1981	AZ 67	**1994**	Ajax
		1982	Ajax	**1995**	Ajax
				1996	Ajax
				1997	PSV Eindhoven
				1998	Ajax
				1999	Feyenoord
				2000	PSV Eindhoven
				2001	PSV Eindhoven
				2002	Ajax
				2003	PSV Eindhoven
				2004	Ajax
				2005	PSV Eindhoven
				2006	PSV Eindhoven
				2007	PSV Eindhoven
				2008	PSV Eindhoven
				2009	AZ
				2010	Twente
				2011	Ajax
				2012	Ajax

1974

1986

OTHER EUROPEAN LEAGUES

These are the other leagues that are ranked highly by UEFA, European football's governing body.

BULGARIA
League: A PFG
Founded: 1924
Most times champions:
CSKA Sofia (31)

CROATIA
League:
Prva HNL
Founded: 1992
Most times champions:
Dinamo Zagreb (14)

CZECH REPUBLIC
League:
Gambrinus Liga
Founded: 1993
Most times champions:
Sparta Prague (11)

DENMARK
League:
Superliga
Founded: 1991
Most times champions:
FC Copenhagen (9)

FINLAND
League:
Veikkausliiga
Founded: 1990
Most times champions:
HJK Helsinki (24)

GREECE
League:
Superleague
Founded: 1927 (2006)
Most times champions:
Olympiacos (39)

ISRAEL
League:
Premier
Founded: 1999
Most times champions:
Maccabi Haifa (7)

NORWAY
League:
Tippeligaen
Founded: 1937 (1991)
Most times champions:
Rosenborg (22)

POLAND
League:
Ekstraklasa
Founded: 1927
Most times champions:
Gornik Zabreze, Wisla Krakow (both 14)

PORTUGAL
League:
Primeira
Founded: 1934
Most times champions:
Benfica (32)

ROMANIA
League: Liga 1
Founded: 1909
Most times champions:
Steaua Bucharest (23)

RUSSIA
League:
Premier
Founded: 2001
Most times champions:
Spartak Moscow (9)

SERBIA
League:
SuperLiga
Founded: 1923 (2006)
Most times champions:
Red Star (25)

SLOVAKIA
League:
Corgon Liga
Founded: 1993
Most times champions: MSK Zilina, Slovan Bratislava (both 6)

SWEDEN
League:
Allsvenskan
Founded: 1924
Most times champions:
Malmo (19)

SWITZERLAND
League:
Super League
Founded: 1897 (2003)
Most times champions:
Grasshopper Zurich (27)

TURKEY
League:
Super Lig
Founded: 1959
Most times champions:
Fenerbahce, Galatasaray (both 18)

UKRAINE
League: Premier
Formed: 1991
Most times champions:
Dynamo Kiev (13)

EUROPEAN CHAMPIONSHIPS

Formerly known as the UEFA European Nations Cup, the European Championships were born in 1968.

Held every four years, the hosts of the event are handed automatic qualification to the tournament.

The other competing teams – 51 began the tournament in 2011-12 – play in a series of qualifying groups to find out which sides will make up the 16 sides in the finals.

There will be 24 finalists from 2016 onwards. The winner of Euro 2012 gains entry to the Confederations Cup.

ALL THE WINNERS...

1960

1960 France
Soviet Union 2 Yugoslavia 1 aet

1964

1964 Spain
Spain 2 Soviet Union 1

1968

1968 Italy
Italy 2 Yugoslavia 0
(After replay, first game 1-1)

EUROPEAN CHAMPIONSHIPS

1972 Belgium
West Germany 3 Soviet Union 0

1984 France
France 2 Spain 0

1976 Yugoslavia
Czechoslovakia 2 West Germany 2
(Czechs 5-3 on penalties)

1988 Germany
Holland 2 Soviet Union 0

1980 Italy
West Germany 2 Belgium 1

1992 Sweden
Denmark 2 Germany 0

1996

1996 England
Germany 2 Czech Republic 1
(Golden goal in extra time)

2000 Holland and Belgium
France 2 Italy 1 *(Golden goal in extra time)*

2004 Portugal
Greece 1 Portugal 0

2010

2008 Austria and Switzerland
Spain 1 Germany 0

2012 Poland and Ukraine
Spain 4 Italy 0

BESTS IN FINALS

MOST GOALS
Michel Platini (France 1984) 9

MOST APPEARANCES
Edin van der Sar (Holland),
Lilian Thuram (France) 16

GOLDEN GOAL SCORERS
Oliver Bierhoff (1996), David Trezeguet (2000)

WORLD CUP

T he 2014 World Cup in Brazil will be the 20th tournament to be played since the competition began back in 1930.

Played every four years, the event took a break during the Second World War.

Although they last won in 2002, Brazil are the kings of the tournament with five wins to their name, ahead of Italy on four and Germany with three.

Thirteen teams took part in the first-ever event but now 32 sides qualify for the finals after taking part in qualifying games staged on six continents around the planet.

ALL THE WINNERS...

1930

1930 Uruguay
Uruguay 4 Argentina 2

1934 Italy
Italy 2 Czechoslovakia 1 (aet)

1938 France
Italy 4 Hungary 2

1950 Brazil
Uruguay 2 Brazil 1

1954 Switzerland
Germany 3 Hungary 2

1958

1958 Sweden
Brazil 5 Sweden 2

1962 Chile
Brazil 3 Czechoslovakia 1

1966 England

England 4 Germany 2 (aet)

Argentina 3 Holland 1 (aet)

1982 Spain

1970 Mexico

Brazil 4 Italy 1

Italy 3 Germany 1

1986 Mexico

1974 Germany

Germany 2 Holland 1

1978 Argentina

Argentina 3 Germany 2

1990 Italy

Germany 1 Argentina 0

1994 USA
Brazil 0 Italy 0 (aet, Brazil 3-2 on penalties)
1998 France

1998

France 3 Brazil 0

2002 Korea-Japan
Brazil 2 Germany 0

2006 Germany
Italy 1 France 1 (aet, Italy 5-3 on penalties)

2010

2010 South Africa
Spain 1 Holland 0 (aet)

FINALS
RECORDS

MOST GOALS TOTAL
Ronaldo (Brazil, 1998-06) 15

MOST GOALS ONE FINALS
Just Fontaine (France, 1958) 13

MOST GOALS ONE MATCH
Oleg Salenko (Russia v Cameroon, 1994) 5

MOST TOURNAMENTS
Antonio Carbajal (Mexico), Lothar
Matthaus (Germany) 5

MOST TITLES
Pele (Brazil, 1958, 1962, 1970) 3

COPA AMERICA

The Copa America is the regional cup for South American federation CONMEBOL.

The tournament was firstly known as the South American Championship before changing to its current name in 1975.

Players such as Pele, Hugo Sanchez and Lionel Messi have all graced this wonderful competition.

The tournament was first held in 1916 – hosted by Argentina and won by Uruguay. Only four teams took part that year and played each other once in a group format. In 1959 there were two championships, one in March and the other in December.

As well as being the first winners Uruguay are also the holders and the most successful nation in the event's 96-year history. In 2011, a brace from Diego Forlan and a Luis Suarez strike helped La Celeste beat Paraguay 3-0 to secure their fifteenth title.

Twelve teams participated in three groups of three with the top two sides and two best third-placed nations advancing to the quarter-finals.

Brazil have captured the trophy the most since its relaunch in 1975, lifting it five times in the last 14 tournaments, while Argentina's Norberto Mendez and Brazil's Zizinho are the Copa's greatest-ever goalscorers with 17 goals.

Guillermo Stabile is the most successful manager, leading Argentina to six South American titles between 1941 and 1957 when it was played every year or two.

Chile will hold the 2015 competition, a year after the World Cup in Brazil.

No qualification system exists as there are only ten teams in the federation.

This leaves two spots free for invited nations – handed to Costa Rica and Mexico in 2011.

ALL THE WINNERS...

1916	Uruguay
1917	Uruguay
1919	Brazil
1920	Uruguay
1921	Argentina
1922	Brazil
1923	Uruguay
1924	Uruguay
1925	Argentina
1926	Uruguay
1927	Argentina
1929	Argentina
1935	Uruguay
1937	Argentina

2011

1939	Peru
1941	Argentina
1942	Uruguay
1945	Argentina
1946	Argentina

1947	Argentina
1949	Brazil
1953	Paraguay
1955	Argentina
1956	Uruguay
1957	Argentina
1959	Argentina
1959	Uruguay
1963	Bolivia
1967	Uruguay

COPA AMERICA

1975	Peru
1979	Paraguay
1983	Uruguay
1987	Uruguay
1989	Brazil
1991	Argentina
1993	Argentina
1995	Uruguay
1997	Brazil
1999	Brazil
2001	Colombia
2004	Brazil
2007	Brazil
2011	Uruguay

2011

AFRICA CUP OF NATIONS

1988

The Africa Cup of Nations is the main international tournament in Africa, hosted by governing body CAF.

It was first organised by Sudan and won by Egypt in 1957. Just three teams took part that year in a straight knockout system.

Due to South Africa's disqualification, Ethiopia got a bye into the final where they were thrashed 4-0 by Egypt. Some 55 years on and 47 teams have to fight it out in a grueling qualification process to become one of the 16 lucky finalists for 2013 in South Africa.

The finals' format is the same as the European Championships – four groups of four, with the top two from each progressing to the knockout stages. Egypt were not just the first winners but also the most successful side, having captured this prestigious title seven times.

Samuel Eto'o is the record scorer with 18 goals. Zambia shocked the world in 2012 when they claimed their first-ever Cup of Nations by defeating favourites Ivory Coast on penalties.

The tournament has often been a stage for players to impress scouts from Europe. Managers Hassan Shehata of Egypt and Charles Gyamfi of Ghana have both lifted the trophy a record three times.

Shehata's victories came in 2006, 2008 and 2010, making his nation the first-ever to win three titles in a row.

ALL THE WINNERS...

1957	Egypt	**1978**	Ghana	**1998**	Egypt
1959	Egypt	**1980**	Nigeria	**2000**	Cameroon
1962	Ethiopia	**1982**	Ghana	**2002**	Cameroon
1963	Ghana	**1984**	Cameroon	**2004**	Tunisia
1965	Ghana	**1986**	Egypt	**2006**	Egypt
1968	Congo-Kinshasa	**1988**	Cameroon	**2008**	Egypt
1970	Sudan	**1990**	Algeria	**2010**	Egypt
1972	Congo-Brazzaville	**1992**	Ivory Coast	**2012**	Zambia
1974	Zaire	**1994**	Nigeria		
1976	Morocco	**1996**	South Africa		

2010

CUPS OF THE

YOUR QUICK GUIDE TO SOME OF THE OTHER TITLES

Spanish Super Cup

Spain's version of the community shield started back in 1982. Barcelona have won the cup a record ten times until the end of 2011-12.

FIFA World Club Championship

Also known as the Club World Cup, it has been contested between the champions from all six continents since 2000. Barcelona are the most successful side with two titles.

CAF Champions League

The African equivalent of the Champions League has been played since 1964. Tunisian outfit ES Tunis were the best of Africa's elite in 2011, while Egypt's Al-Ahly SC have won the title a record six times.

Copa Libertadores

South America's Libertadores is broadcast in 135 countries and has a 52-year history. Argentina's Independiente have won a record seven times and Santos from Brazil are the 2011-12 holders.

AFC Champions League

Asia's Premier club competition was first held in 1967. Korea's Pohang Steelers have a record three victories and Al-Sadd won it in 2011.

OFC Champions League

Oceania's elite competition is the youngest of all the continents having first been played in 1987. Australia's Auckland City are the current champions and most successful side with four titles.

Asian Cup

The competition started in 1956 and runs every four years to find the champions of Asia. Current holders Japan have won a record four titles.

WORLD

AND TROPHIES ON OFFER AROUND THE PLANET

CONCACAF Champions League
Twenty-four clubs battle it out to be crowned best club side in the CONCACAF region. Mexican sides Cruz Azul and Club America are both the most successful with five titles.

CONCACAF Gold Cup
This international tournament, played since 1991, is between 12 international teams in the Caribbean plus North and Central America. Mexico have claimed the prize a record six times.

Irish Cup
A knockout competition for all clubs in Northern Ireland. Linfield beat Crusaders 4-1 in the 2012 final for their undefeated 42nd title.

FAI Cup
The Republic of Ireland's cup sees 45 teams go head-to-head in a straight knockout format. Shamrock Rovers have a record 24 wins.

Johnstone's Paint Trophy
This competition features just League One and League Two clubs. Carlisle, Birmingham City, Blackpool, Bristol City, Port Vale, Stoke, Swansea and Wigan have all won it twice.

Welsh Cup
Wrexham have won this title a record 23 times, but have not been allowed to participate since 1996 because they ply their trade in the English leagues.

FIFA Confederations Cup
The six holders of each continental championship, the World Champions and the host battle for this cup. It is played in the country that's a year away from hosting the World Cup. Brazil have three titles.

MANAGER
OF SEASON
THE

2011-12

The Premier League Manager of the Season award didn't start until after the second season of the competition.

But it didn't really matter – as Manchester United's Sir Alex Ferguson won the trophy having guided his side to a second successive title.

Ferguson has dominated the awards as his team have picked up title-after-title but other managers who have not won the league have been recognised by the panel who make the accolade.

In 2001 George Burley lifted the crown for guiding Ipswich to fifth; 2010 saw Harry Redknapp land the award for taking Spurs to fourth and into the Champions League for the first time; 2012's winner was Alan Pardew who turned around Newcastle's fortunes and took them to fifth.

ALL THE WINNERS...

1993-94 Alex Ferguson (Manchester United)	**2003-04** Arsene Wenger (Arsenal)
1994-95 Kenny Dalglish (Blackburn Rovers)	**2004-05** Jose Mourinho (Chelsea)
1995-96 Alex Ferguson (Manchester United)	**2005-06** Jose Mourinho (Chelsea)
1996-97 Alex Ferguson (Manchester United)	**2006-07** Alex Ferguson (Manchester United)
1997-98 Arsene Wenger (Arsenal)	**2007-08** Alex Ferguson (Manchester United)
1998-99 Alex Ferguson (Manchester United)	**2008-09** Alex Ferguson (Manchester United)
1999-00 Alex Ferguson (Manchester United)	**2009-10** Harry Redknapp (Tottenham)
2000-01 George Burley (Ipswich Town)	**2010-11** Alex Ferguson (Manchester United)
2001-02 Arsene Wenger (Arsenal)	**2011-12** Alan Pardew (Newcastle United)
2002-03 Alex Ferguson (Manchester United)	

2004-05

2003-04

MANAGER
OF THE MONTH

The Premier League Manager of the Month award started in August 1993 and the first one went to Sir Alex Ferguson at Manchester United. Until the end of season 2011-12 some 31 managers had won the award more than once:

26 Alex Ferguson (Man United)
12 Arsene Wenger (Arsenal)
8 David Moyes (Everton)
8 Martin O'Neill (Leicester, Aston Villa, Sunderland)
8 Harry Redknapp (West Ham, Portsmouth, Southampton, Tottenham)
6 Bobby Robson (Newcastle United)
6 Rafael Benitez (Liverpool)
5 Kevin Keegan (Newcastle United)
4 Sam Allardyce (Bolton)
4 Carlo Ancelotti (Chelsea)
4 Roy Hodgson (Blackburn Rovers, Fulham)
4 Joe Kinnear (Wimbledon)
4 Gordon Strachan (Coventry, Southampton)
3 Alan Curbishley (Charlton)
3 Gerard Houllier (Liverpool)
3 Jose Mourinho (Chelsea)
3 David O'Leary (Leeds)
Stuart Pearce (Nottingham Forest, Man City)
2 Frank Clark (Nottingham Forest)
2 Steve Coppell (Reading)
2 Kenny Dalglish (Blackburn Rovers)
Roy Evans (Liverpool)
2 John Gregory (Aston Villa)
Glenn Hoddle (Tottenham)
Paul Jewell (Wigan)
Roberto Mancini (Man City)
Owen Coyle (Bolton)
Claudio Ranieri (Chelsea)
Peter Reid (Sunderland)
Graeme Souness (Southampton)
Phil Thomson (Liverpool)

1994

LMA MANAGER
OF THE YEAR

The League Managers' Association also hand out an award to their boss of the year. It is voted for by other managers.

1994	Joe Kinnear (Wimbledon)
1995	Frank Clark (Nottingham Forest)
1996	Peter Reid (Sunderland)
1997	Danny Wilson (Barnsley)
1998	Dave Jones (Southampton)
1999	Alex Ferguson (Man United)
2000	Alan Curbishley (Charlton)
2001	George Burley (Ipswich Town)
2002	Arsene Wenger (Arsenal)
2003	David Moyes (Everton)
2004	Arsene Wenger (Arsenal)
2005	David Moyes (Everton)
2006	Steve Coppell (Reading)
2007	Steve Coppell (Reading)
2008	Alex Ferguson (Man United)
2009	David Moyes (Everton)
2010	Roy Hodgson (Fulham)
2011	Alex Ferguson (Man United)
2012	Alan Pardew (Newcastle United)

England Managers' Records

Roy Hodgson became the sixteenth manager of England when he took over on May 1, 2012. Sir Alf Ramsey won the 1966 World Cup but the stats show Italian Fabio Capello is currently the most successful boss.

Sir Walter **Winterbottom**
1946-63

RECORD: Played 139 **Won** 78 **Drew** 33 **Lost** 28

Winterbottom was the first manager appointed by England and was in charge for more than half of the matches played so far by the national side. Until his appointment FA officials selected the team.

Joe **Mercer**
1974

RECORD: Played 7 **Won** 3 **Drew** 3 **Lost** 1

Whilst managing Coventry City, Mercer took on the role of England caretaker and jointly won the Home Championships with Scotland. Had previously been boss at Sheffield United, Aston Villa and Manchester City.

Sir Alf **Ramsey**
1963-74

RECORD: Played 113 **Won** 69 **Drew** 27 **Lost** 17

Guided England to World Cup victory at Wembley in 1966 and was in charge of the team until 1974. Departed amid reports that he was not the most popular man within the FA.

Don **Revie**
1974-77

RECORD: Played 29 **Won** 14 **Drew** 8 **Lost** 7

The all-conquering boss of Leeds United during their glory years of the late 1960s and early 1970s, Revie was an obvious choice for national team manager. He failed to qualify for the 1976 Euros or 1978 World Cup and caused uproar by quitting to coach the United Arab Emirates.

Ron **Greenwood**
1977-82

RECORD: Played 55 **Won** 33 **Drew** 12 **Lost** 10

A success with West Ham United during 13 years as boss at Upton Park, Greenwood was an obvious successor to Revie. He took the Three Lions to the European Championship in 1980 and World Cup in 1982. He then resigned, leaving football altogether.

Sir Bobby **Robson**
1982-90

RECORD: Played 95 **Won** 47 **Drew** 30 **Lost** 18

Success with Ipswich got Sir Bobby the job yet he came under attack for poor results. Led England to the Italia '90 penalty shoot-out having announced his decision to leave before that World Cup. Enjoyed success in Holland, Portugal and Spain before revitalising boyhood club Newcastle.

Graham **Taylor**
1990-93

RECORD: Played 38 **Won** 18 **Drew** 13 **Lost** 7

Taylor was the rising star English football when he took on the job, having had major success with Watford under pop star chairman Elton John. Taylor has since admitted that he simply could not refuse the position but probably needed more experience at club level before taking on the role.

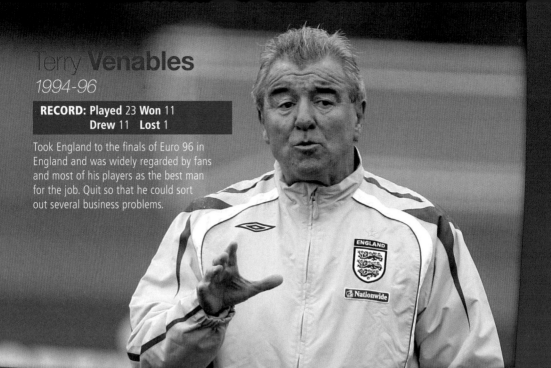

Terry **Venables**
1994-96

RECORD: Played 23 **Won** 11
Drew 11 **Lost** 1

Took England to the finals of Euro 96 in England and was widely regarded by fans and most of his players as the best man for the job. Quit so that he could sort out several business problems.

Glenn **Hoddle**
1996-99

RECORD: Played 28 **Won** 17 **Drew** 6 **Lost** 5

The signs were good for the former Tottenham and Monaco midfielder until a few badly chosen words in a newspaper interview cost him his job.

Howard **Wilkinson**
1999-00

RECORD: Played 2 **Won** 0 **Drew** 1 **Lost** 1

The last English manager to win the top-flight title in England –with Leeds United – stood in as caretaker as part of his duties with the FA.

Kevin **Keegan**
1999-00

RECORD: Played 18 **Won** 7 **Drew** 7 **Lost** 4

The people's choice to take over as boss but not for the first time walked away from a job. Quit after England lost the last-ever game at Wembley to old rivals Germany. Has said there should be an overseas manager.

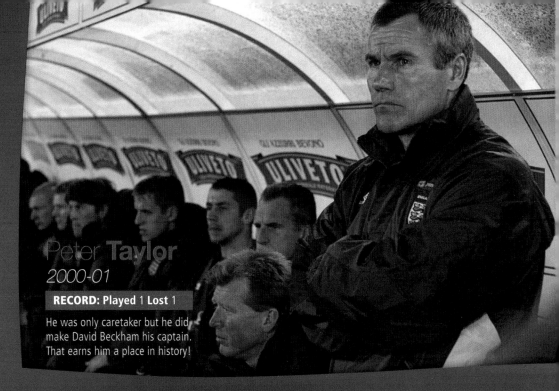

Peter **Taylor**
2000-01

RECORD: Played 1 **Lost** 1

He was only caretaker but he did make David Beckham his captain. That earns him a place in history!

Sven **Goran Eriksson**
2001-06

RECORD: Played 67 **Won** 40 **Drew** 17 **Lost** 10

The Three Lions' first overseas manager took them to World Cup 2002, Euro 2004 and World Cup 2006. England reached the quarter-finals in all three of those tournaments. He was released from his contract by mutual consent after Germany 2006.

Steve **McClaren**
2006-07

RECORD: Played 18 **Won** 9 **Drew** 4 **Lost** 5

Having gained a reputation as a good coach working under Sir Alex Ferguson at Manchester United, McClaren took over as Middlesbrough manager. He guided Boro to their first major trophy, the 2004 League Cup. England proved a step too far – but he went to Holland and won the Eredivisie title with Twente.

Fabio **Capello**
2007-12

RECORD: Played 42 **Won** 28 **Drew** 8 **Lost** 6

The Italian took over after an impressive club management record in his home country and with Real Madrid. He took England to the 2010 World Cup finals where they were disappointingly knocked out in the second round. Having reached the finals of Euro 2012 he resigned just months before the tournament when the FA removed John Terry as captain.

ENGLISH FOOTBALL
HALL OF FAME

The National Football Museum in Manchester is the home of football's Hall of Fame. The greatest players, leading managers and top teams have all earned their places and each year a selection panel adds more names to the list of entries. There are also a number of special awards handed out every year. These are the noted players and managers…

Colin Bell

Played more than 580 club games between 1963 and 1979, most for Manchester City. Won 48 England caps and scored nine international goals.

PLAYERS

Tony Adams	**Cliff Bastin**	**Danny**	**Trevor Brooking**
Jimmy Armfield	**Peter Beardsley**	**Blanchflower**	**Charlie Buchan**
Alan Ball	**David Beckham**	**Steve Bloomer**	**Ian Callaghan**
Gordon Banks	**Dennis Bergkamp**	**Liam Brady**	**Eric Cantona**
John Barnes	**George Best**	**Billy Bremner**	**Bobby Charlton**

Viv Anderson

The first black player to turn out for England, Anderson earned 30 caps. He lifted the league with Nottingham Forest and the European Cup in 1979 and 1980. In a career from 1974 to 1995 he also played for Arsenal, Man United, Sheffield Wednesday, Barnsley and Middlesbrough.

Martin Peters

A scorer in England's 1966 World Cup victory, midfielder Peters played his club football from 1959 to 1981. The bulk of his games were with West Ham but he also turned out for Tottenham, Norwich City and Sheffield United.

Jack Charlton	Peter Doherty	Ryan Giggs	Thierry Henry
Ray Clemence	Duncan Edwards	Johnny Giles	Glenn Hoddle
George Cohen	Tom Finney	Jimmy Greaves	Emlyn Hughes
Kenny Dalglish	Paul Gascoigne	Alan Hansen	Mark Hughes
Dixie Dean	Steven Gerrard	Johnny Hayes	Roger Hunt

Ossie Ardiles

A World Cup-winner in 1978 with Argentina, midfielder Ardiles won 63 caps. Made his name in England with Tottenham between 1978-88 when he won two FA Cups and the UEFA Cup.

PLAYERS Cont...

Geoff Hurst	Denis Law	Dave Mackay	Jackie Milburn
Alex James	Tommy Lawton	Frank McLintock	Bobby Moore
Pat Jennings	Francis Lee	Wilf Mannion	Stan Mortensen
Roy Keane	Gary Lineker	Stanley Matthews	Alf Ramsey
Kevin Keegan	Nat Lofthouse	Billy Meredith	Bryan Robson

John Charles

Regarded as one of Wales' finest, played both in defence and attack and won 38 caps. Between 1948 and 1971 he played for Leeds United, Juventus, Roma, Cardiff City and Hereford United.

Ian Rush	Teddy Sheringham	Nobby Stiles	Billy Wright
Peter Schmeichel	Peter Shilton	Frank Swift	Ian Wright
Paul Scholes	Graeme Souness	Bert Trautmann	Gianfranco Zola
Len Shackleton	Neville Southall	Arthur Wharton	
Alan Shearer	Clem Stephenson	Ray Wilson	

Brian Clough

A striker whose career was cut short by injury, Clough carved out a successful career as a boss and won back-to-back European Cups at Nottingham Forest

MANAGERS

Malcolm Allison	**Herbert Chapman**	**Ron Greenwood**
Matt Busby	**Stan Cullis**	**Howard Kendall**
Harry Catterick	**Alex Ferguson**	**Bertie Mee**

Bill Nicholson

A Tottenham player from 1938-55 and then the club's manager from 1958-74. Nicholson played 341 games for Spurs and won the league title as both a player and manager. As boss he also won three FA Cups, two League Cups, the Cup Winner's Cup and UEFA Cup. Died in 2004 at the age of 85.

Dario Gradi

After spells as manager at Wimbledon and Crystal Palace, Gradi joined Crewe Alexandra in 1983 and is still with them. He was boss of Alex for more than 1,200 games. He is regarded as one of the country's best developers of young talent. A street in the town has been named in his honour.

Joe Mercer	**Don Revie**	**Terry Venables**
Bob Paisley	**Bobby Robson**	**Arsene Wenger**
Alf Ramsey	**Bill Shankly**	**Walter Winterbottom**

WORLD PLAYERS OF THE YEAR

Since 1991 coaches and captains of international teams have voted for their World Player of the Year. In 2010 this award was merged with the Ballon d'Or to create one award, the FIFA Ballon d'Or.

1991
Lothar Mattaus
Germany
Inter Milan

1992
Marco van Basten
Holland
AC Milan

1993
Roberto Baggio
Italy
Juventus

1994
Romario
Brazil
Barcelona

1995
George Weah
Liberia
AC Milan

1996
Ronaldo
Brazil
Barcelona

1997
Ronaldo
Brazil
Inter Milan

1998
Zinedine Zidane
France
Juventus

1999
Rivaldo
Brazil
Barcelona

2000
Zinedine Zidane
France
Juventus

2001
Luis Figo
Portugal
Real Madrid

2002
Ronaldo
Brazil
Real Madrid

2003
Zinedine Zidane
France
Real Madrid

2004
Ronaldinho
Brazil
Barcelona

2005
Ronaldinho
Brazil
Barcelona

2006
Fabio Cannavaro
Italy
Real Madrid

2007
Kaka
Brazil
AC Milan

2008
Cristiano Ronaldo
Portugal
Manchester United

2009
Lionel Messi
Argentina
Barcelona

2010
Lionel Messi
Argentina
Barcelona

2011
Lionel Messi
Argentina
Barcelona

BALLON D'OR

The Ballon d'Or was often referred to as the European Footballer of the Year award. It was created in 1956 by France Football magazine but in 2010 it was merged with FIFA's World Player of the Year to become the FIFA Ballon D'Or and is awarded to the world's best player that campaign.

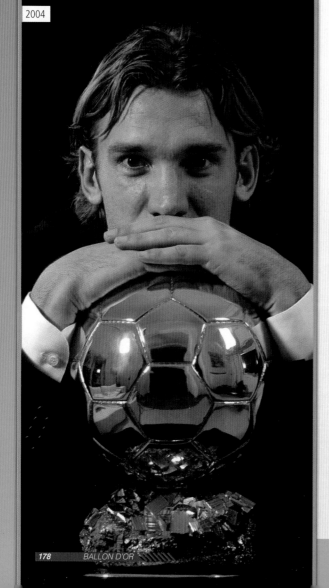

2004

ALL THE WINNERS...

1956   Stanley Matthews (England)

1956

1957   Alfredo Di Stefano (Argentina)
1958   Raymond Kopa (France)
1959   Alfredo Di Stefano (Argentina)
1960   Luis Suarez (Spain)
1961   Omar Sivori (Italy)
1962   Josef Masopust (Czechoslovaki)
1963   Lev Yashin (Soviet Union)
1964   Denis Law (Scotland)
1965   Eusebio (Portugal)

1965

1966   Bobby Charlton (England)
1967   Florian Albert (Hungary)
1968   George Best (Northern Ireland)
1969   Gianni Rivera (Italy)
1970   Gerd Müller (Germany)

1971	Johan Cruyff (Holland)	1986	Igor Belanov (Soviet Union)
1972	Franz Beckenbauer (Germany)	1987	Ruud Gullit (Holland)
1973	Johan Cruyff (Holland)	1988	Marco Van Basten (Holland)
1974	Johan Cruyff (Holland)	1989	Marco Van Basten (Holland)
1975	Oleg Blokhin (Soviet Union)	1990	Lothar Matthaus (Germany)
1976	Franz Beckenbauer (Germany)	1991	Jean-Pierre Papin (France)
1977	Allan Simonsen (Denmark)	1992	Marco Van Basten (Holland)
1978	Kevin Keegan (England)	1993	Roberto Baggio (Italy)

1986 Igor Belanov (Soviet Union)
1987 Ruud Gullit (Holland)
1988 Marco Van Basten (Holland)
1989 Marco Van Basten (Holland)
1990 Lothar Matthaus (Germany)
1991 Jean-Pierre Papin (France)
1992 Marco Van Basten (Holland)
1993 Roberto Baggio (Italy)
1994 Hristo Stoichkov (Bulgaria)
1995 George Weah (Liberia)
1996 Matthias Sammer (Germany)
1997 Ronaldo (Brazil)
1998 Zinedine Zidane (France)
1999 Rivaldo (Brazil)
2000 Luis Figo (Portugal)
2001 Michael Owen (England)

1978

1979 Kevin Keegan (England)
1980 Karl-Heinz Rummenigge (Germany)
1981 Karl-Heinz Rummenigge (Germany)
1982 Paolo Rossi (Italy)
1983 Michel Platini (France)
1984 Michel Platini (France)

2001

1984

2002 Ronaldo (Brazil)
2003 Pavel Nedved (Czech Republic)
2004 Andriy Shevchenko (Ukraine)
2005 Ronaldinho (Brazil)
2006 Fabio Cannavaro (Italy)
2007 Kaka (Brazil)
2008 Cristiano Ronaldo (Portugal)
2009 Lionel Messi (Argentina)
(See pages 176-177 for combined award winners from 2010 onwards)

1985 Michel Platini (France)

PFA PLAYER OF THE YEAR

T he Professional Footballers' Association – the players' union – has presented its Players' Player of the Year award since 1974. The awards are highly prized as all professional players have a vote.

2010

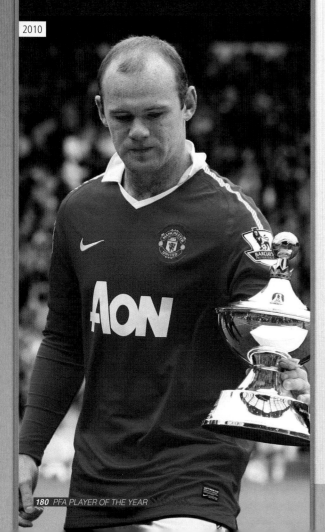

ALL THE WINNERS..

1974 Norman Hunter (Leeds United)
1975 Colin Todd (Derby County)
1976 Pat Jennings (Tottenham)

1976

1977 Andy Gray (Aston Villa)
1978 Peter Shilton (Nottingham Forest)
1979 Liam Brady (Arsenal)
1980 Terry McDermott (Liverpool)
1981 John Wark (Ipswich Town)
1982 Kevin Keegan (Southampton)
1983 Kenny Dalglish (Liverpool)
1984 Ian Rush (Liverpool)
1985 Peter Reid (Everton)
1986 Gary Lineker (Everton)
1987 Clive Allen (Tottenham)
1988 John Barnes (Liverpool)
1989 Mark Hughes (Manchester United)
1990 David Platt (Aston Villa)
1991 Mark Hughes (Manchester United)
1992 Gary Pallister (Manchester United)
1993 Paul McGrath (Aston Villa)
1994 Eric Cantona (Manchester United)
1995 Alan Shearer (Blackburn Rovers)
1996 Les Ferdinand (Newcastle United)
1997 Alan Shearer (Newcastle United)
1998 Dennis Bergkamp (Arsenal)
1999 David Ginola (Tottenham)
2000 Roy Keane (Manchester United)
2001 Teddy Sheringham (Manchester United)
2002 Ruud van Nistelrooy (Manchester United)
2003 Thierry Henry (Arsenal)

2004 Thierry Henry (Arsenal)

2004

2005 John Terry (Chelsea)
2006 Steven Gerrard (Liverpool)
2007 Cristiano Ronaldo (Manchester United)
2008 Cristiano Ronaldo (Manchester United)
2009 Ryan Giggs (Manchester United)
2010 Wayne Rooney (Manchester United)
2011 Gareth Bale (Tottenham)
2012 Robin van Persie (Arsenal)

2012

YOUNG PLAYER
OF THE YEAR...

1974 Kevin Beattie (Ipswich Town)
1975 Mervyn Day (West Ham)
1976 Peter Barnes (Manchester City)
1977 Andy Gray (Aston Villa)
1978 Tony Woodcock (Nottingham Forest)
1979 Cyrille Regis (West Brom)
1980 Glenn Hoddle (Tottenham)
1981 Gary Shaw (Aston Villa)
1982 Steve Moran (Southampton)
1983 Ian Rush (Liverpool)

1984 Paul Walsh (Luton Town)
1985 Mark Hughes (Manchester United)
1986 Tony Cottee (West Ham)
1987 Tony Adams (Arsenal)
1988 Paul Gascoigne (Newcastle United)
1989 Paul Merson (Arsenal)
1990 Matt Le Tissier (Southampton)
1991 Lee Sharpe (Manchester United)
1992 Ryan Giggs (Manchester United)
1993 Ryan Giggs (Manchester United)
1994 Andy Cole (Newcastle United)
1995 Robbie Fowler (Liverpool)
1996 Robbie Fowler (Liverpool)
1997 David Beckham (Manchester United)
1998 Michael Owen (Liverpool)
1999 Nicolas Anelka (Arsenal)
2000 Harry Kewell (Leeds United)
2001 Steven Gerrard (Liverpool)
2002 Craig Bellamy (Newcastle United)
2003 Jermaine Jenas (Newcastle United)
2004 Scott Parker (Charlton Athletic/Chelsea)
2005 Wayne Rooney (Manchester United)
2006 Wayne Rooney (Manchester United)
2007 Cristiano Ronaldo (Manchester United)
2008 Cesc Fabregas (Arsenal)
2009 Ashley Young (Aston Villa)
2010 James Milner (Aston Villa)
2011 Jack Wilshere (Arsenal)
2012 Kyle Walker (Tottenham)

2012

FWA
FOOTBALLER
OF THE YEAR

The Football Writers' Association Footballer of the Year Award was created back in 1947-48. Charles Buchan, famed as the publisher of *Football Monthly*, had suggested the honour should be voted for by association members.

2012

ALL THE WINNERS...

1948 Stanley Matthews (Blackpool)
1949 Johnny Carey (Manchester United)
1950 Joe Mercer (Arsenal)
1951 Harry Johnston (Blackpool)
1952 Billy Wright (Wolves)
1953 Nat Lofthouse (Bolton)
1954 Tom Finney (Preston North End)
1955 Don Revie (Manchester City)
1956 Bert Trautmann (Manchester City)
1957 Tom Finney (Preston North End)
1958 Danny Blanchflower (Tottenham)
1959 Syd Owen (Luton Town)
1960 Bill Slater (Wolves)

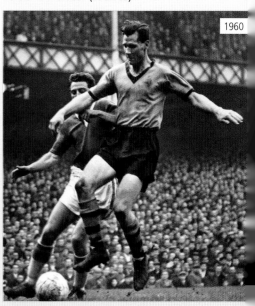

1960

1961 Danny Blanchflower (Tottenham)
1962 Jimmy Adamson (Burnley)
1963 Stanley Matthews (Stoke City)
1964 Bobby Moore (West Ham)
1965 Bobby Collins (Leeds United)
1966 Bobby Charlton (Manchester United)
1967 Jack Charlton (Leeds United)
1968 George Best (Manchester United)
1969 Tony Book (Manchester City)
     and Dave Mackay (Derby County)

1970 Billy Bremner (Leeds United)
1971 Frank McLintock (Arsenal)
1972 Gordon Banks (Stoke City)
1973 Pat Jennings (Tottenham)
1974 Ian Callaghan (Liverpool)
1975 Alan Mullery (Fulham)
1976 Kevin Keegan (Liverpool)
1977 Emlyn Hughes (Liverpool)
1978 Kenny Burns (Nottingham Forest)
1979 Kenny Dalglish (Liverpool)
1980 Terry McDermott (Liverpool)
1981 Frans Thijssen (Ipswich Town)
1982 Steve Perryman (Tottenham)
1983 Kenny Dalglish (Liverpool)
1984 Ian Rush (Liverpool)
1985 Neville Southall (Everton)
1986 Gary Lineker (Everton)
1987 Clive Allen (Tottenham)
1988 John Barnes (Liverpool)
1989 Steve Nicol (Liverpool)
1990 John Barnes (Livepool)

1990

1991 Gordon Strachan (Leeds United)
1992 Gary Lineker (Tottenham)

1993 Chris Waddle (Sheffield Wednesday)
1994 Alan Shearer (Blackburn Rovers)

1994

1995 Jurgen Klinsmann (Tottenham)
1996 Eric Cantona (Manchester United)
1997 Gianfranco Zola (Chelsea)
1998 Dennis Bergkamp (Arsenal)
1999 David Ginola (Tottenham)
2000 Roy Keane (Manchester United)
2001 Teddy Sheringham (Manchester United)
2002 Robert Pires (Arsenal)
2003 Thierry Henry (Arsenal)
2004 Thierry Henry (Arsenal)
2005 Frank Lampard (Chelsea)
2006 Thierry Henry (Arsenal)
2007 Cristiano Ronaldo (Manchester United)
2008 Cristiano Ronaldo (Manchester United)
2009 Steven Gerrard (Liverpool)
2010 Wayne Rooney (Manchester United)
2011 Scott Parker (West Ham)
2012 Robin van Persie (Arsenal)

TOP TEN RECORDS

Most titles

1. **Rangers** (Scotland) 54
2. **Linfield** (Ireland) 51
3. **Penarol** (Uruguay) 48
4. **Olimpia** (Paraguay) 39
5. **Olympiacos** (Greece) 39
6. **Al Ahly** (Egypt) 36
7. **River Plate** (Argentina) 34
8. **Benfica** (Portugal) 32
9. **Rapid Vienna** (Austria) 32
10. **Al-Muharraq Club** (Bahrain) 32
    Real Madrid (Spain) 32

Most goals in one season

1. **Lionel Messi,** Barcelona	2011-12	73
2. **Gerd Muller,** Bayern Munich	1972-73	67
3. **Ferenc Deak,** Szentlorinc	1945-46	66
4. **Gyula Zsengeller,** Ujpest	1938-39	65
5. **Dixie Dean,** Everton	1927-28	63
6. **Jimmy McGrory,** Celtic	1927-28	63
7. **Cristiano Ronaldo,** Real Madrid	2011-12	60
8. **Ferenc Deak,** Ferencvaros	1948-49	59
9. **Refik Resmja,** Partizani Tirana	1950-51	59
Fred Roberts, Glentoran	1930-31	59
Jimmy McGrory, Celtic	1926-27	59

Transfer fees

1. **Cristiano Ronaldo**
   Manchester United > Real Madrid, 2009 £80m
2. **Zlatan Ibrahimovic**
   Inter Milan > Barcelona, 2009 £60.7m
3. **Kaka**
   Inter Milan > Barcelona, 2009 £56m
4. **Fernando Torres**
   Liverpool > Chelsea, 2011 £50m
5. **Zinedine Zidane**
   Juventus > Real Madrid, 2001 £45m
6. **Luis Figo**
   Barcelona > Real Madrid, 2000 £37m
7. **Javier Pastore**
   Palermo > Paris Saint German, 2011 £36.7m
8. **Hernan Crespo**
   Parma > Lazio, 2000 £35.5m
9. **Radamel Falcao**
   Porto > Atletico Madrid, 2011 £35.2m
10. **Sergio Aguero**
    Atletico Madrid > Manchester City 2011 £35m
    Andy Carroll
    Newcastle United > Liverpool 2011 £35m

Top scorers in European competition

1. **Raul** 75
2. **Filippo Inzaghi** 70
3. **Gerd Muller** 69
4. **Andriy Schevchenko** 67
5. **Ruud van Nistelrooy** 62
6. **Henrik Larsson** 59
7. **Thierry Henry** 59
8. **Eusebio** 58
9. **Alessandro del Piero** 53
10. **Lionel Messi** 52

FASTEST GOALS

Premier League

Fastest goal: Ledley King
(Tottenham) v Bradford City 2000 10 seconds
Fastest hat-trick: Robbie Fowler
(Liverpool) v Arsenal, 1994 4m 33 secs
As a sub: Nicklas Bendtner
(Arsenal) v Tottenham 2007 1.8 seconds

Football League

Fastest hat-trick: James Hayter
(Bournemouth) v Wrexham 2004 2 mins 20 seconds
Debut goal: Freddy Eastwood
(Southend) v Swansea 2004 7 seconds

FA Cup Final

Louis Saha (Everton) v Chelsea 2009 25 seconds

League Cup Final

John Arne Riise
(Liverpool) v Chelsea 2005 45 seconds

European Cup

Roy Makaay
(Bayern Munich) v Real Madrid, 2007 10.2 seconds

European Championships

Dmitri Kirichenko
(Russia) v Greece 2004 67 seconds

World Cup Finals

Hakan Sukur
(Turkey) v South Korea 2002 11 seconds

Fastest goals ever

Nawaf Al Abed
(Al Hilal) v Al Shoalah 2009 2 seconds
Ricardo Olivera
(Rio Negro) v Soriano 1998 2.8 seconds
Damian Mori
(Adelaide City) v Sydney United 1995 3.5 seconds

VARIOUS RECORDS

English league appearances

1,005 Peter Shilton, 1966-97
931 Tony Ford, 1975-02
909 Graeme Armstrong, 1975-01
863 Tommy Hutchison, 1965-91
833 Graham Alexander, 1991-12
824 Terry Paine, 1957-77
790 Neil Readfearn, 1982-04
782 Robbie James, 1973-94
777 Alan Oakes, 1959-84
774 Dave Beasant, 1979-03
771 John Burridge, 1968-96
770 John Trollope, 1960-80

Big scores

Arbroath 36 Bon Accord 0, Scottish Cup 1885
Dundee Harp 35 Aberdeen Rovers 0,
Scottish Cup 1885
Australia 31 American Samoa 0,
World Cup qualifier, 2001
Villarreal 27 Navata 0, friendly, 2009
*   John Petrie (Arbroath) and Archie Thompson
      (Australia) both scored 13 goals in the games
      mentioned above to set a joint world record.
** In English local football the record scores are
      thought to include Wheel Power 58 Nova 0
      (Torquay Sunday League, 2012) and Illogan 55
      Madron 0 (Mining Football League 2010).

Speed merchants

All these guys will claim they are the fastest – or were the fastest in their prime! Here are some of the speediest footballers on the planet and their claimed 100m times in seconds…

Theo Walcott (Arsenal) 10.3
Obafemi Martins (Rubin Kazan) 10.6
Cristiano Ronaldo (Real Madrid) 10.63
Ryo Miyaichi (Arsenal) 10.84
Gabriel Agbonlahor (Aston Villa) 10.98
Javier Hernandez (Man United) 11.08
Nedum Onuoha (QPR) 11.09
Cha Du-Ri (Fortuna Dusseldorf) 11.2
Arjen Robben (Bayern Munich) 11.34
Gareth Bale (Tottenham) 11.39
Antonio Valencia (Man United) 11.45
Robin Van Persie (Arsenal) 11.54